PRAISE FOR *The End of Nature*

"Whatever we once thought Nature was—wildness, God, a simple place free from human thumbprints, or an intricate machinery sustaining life on Earth—we have now given it a kick that will change it forever. Humanity has stepped across a threshold. In his free-ranging and provocative book, Bill McKibben explores the philosophies and technologies that have brought us here, and he shows how final a crossing we have made."

—JAMES GLEICK, author of *Chaos*

"By the end of nature Mr. McKibben means the end of nature as a force independent of man. . . . For a man preaching apocalypse, he speaks in a measured and civilized voice that deserves a hearing."

—*The New York Times Book Review*

"*The End of Nature* is not another doomsday book. McKibben does not forecast the end of man but the end of a primal relationship. . . . It is almost impossible for a reader to walk away from this book and not reassess his relationship with a world where rapid growth and smog make it harder each night to see the stars."

—*Daily News* (Los Angeles)

"[*The End of Nature*] will probably become the critical text for intelligent environmentalism in the next decade."

—*The Independent* (London)

"Like Aldo Leopold, Rachel Carson and Jonathan Schell, McKibben belongs to that rare breed of writer who will take an honest look at what we have done to the earth. *The End of Nature* is his brave attempt to record some of the consequences of our folly."

—*Albuquerque Sunday Journal*

"This is a thoughtful book by a fine writ

The End of Nature

For Nathan —

think globally,

act

neighborly!

B.

350.org

The End of
NATURE

Bill McKibben

RANDOM HOUSE TRADE PAPERBACKS
NEW YORK

LIBRARY OF CONGRESS CATALOGING-IN-PUBLICATION DATA
McKibben, Bill.
The end of nature / Bill McKibben.
p.   cm.
ISBN 0-8129-7608-8
I. Man—Influence on nature.   2. Greenhouse effect, Atmospheric.
3. Environmental protection.   I. Title.
[GF75.M38   1990]
304.2'8—dc20   90-34480

Acknowledgments

I OWE A LARGE DEBT—all of us owe a large debt—to the scientists who have brought to the world's attention the greenhouse effect and the other environmental cataclysms described in this book. The science of global climate change is young and still evolving, so there are few textbooks or standard references on which to draw. However, the investigators in this field have made many efforts to communicate their findings to the public, and much of the most important material has been collected in several government reports, the most recent of which is *Policy Options for Stabilizing Global Climate*, a two-volume report to Congress from the Environmental Protection Agency. Other important summaries have been issued by the National Research Council, the National Academy of Sciences, and the United Nations.

I am indebted to a number of individual scientists and policy analysts, who helped me understand the implications of their work. This list includes, among many others, James Hansen, Roger Revelle, Stephen Schneider, George Woodwell, Pat Zimmerman, Michael McElroy, Irving Mintzer, and James Titus. Many of these researchers work at government agencies or universities, while others are employed by a constellation of nonprofit environmental groups whose reports have helped me considerably. These groups include the Worldwatch Institute (which publishes a valuable planetary "checkup" each year), the World Resources Institute (which conducts extensive independent policy analysis), the Environmental Policy Institute (which has done a particularly good job addressing the ozone question), the Natural Resources Defense Council, the Environmental Defense Fund, and others. None of them, of course, is responsible for my characterizations of their work.

As much of this work deals with society's response to global change, I have made extensive use of the popular press—*The New York Times* in particular has kept me abreast of developments, and I have also relied on magazines as far afield as the *New Statesman* and *International Wildlife*. The Southern Adirondack Library System tracked down some of the more obscure naturalist writings that I have quoted, while others have recently become more easily available in a series of "Penguin Nature Library" reprints, edited by Edward Hoagland. Paul Brooks's fine summary of American nature writing helped order my thinking.

For additional help in gathering material, I am indebted to Robert Silvers, editor of the *New York Review of Books*, who also provided me with a forum to try out some of the material in the opening chapter. His assistants—Henning Gutmann, Neil Gordon, and Ann Kjellberg—were also of great assistance.

The Lyndhurst Foundation helped support this work, and for their aid to both my finances and morale I am very thankful.

Gloria Loomis, my agent, did a marvelous job of finding this book a home; I thank both her and Kendra Taylor, her assistant.

For their valuable early readings of my manuscript, I am indebted to David Edelstein, Scott Rosenberg, Sam and Lisa Verhovek, David Goldfarb, Shawn Leary, and Bill Finnegan. David Rosenthal, my editor at Random House, improved my original efforts immeasurably, chipping away at the blocks of verbal stone in which I had imprisoned my argument until its outlines became more visible. His colleagues at Random House—Joni Evans, Annik LaFarge, Sono Rosenberg, Mitchell Ivers, Mary Peters, Jennifer Ash, and many others—were also of great assistance, as was Tim Guzley, who checked the facts contained herein.

Many at the *New Yorker* magazine aided my efforts—especially

Sara Lippincott and the incomparable Eleanor Gould Packard, as well as the checking staff led by Martin Baron.

My neighbors, especially the men and women of the Johnsburg United Methodist Church and our pastor, Rev. Lucy B. Hathaway, were a great support and resource. My parents, Peggy and Gordon McKibben, besides their obvious crucial role in any effort of mine, also shuttled much information back to me from their London home. My brother, Tom, provided a good deal of spirited criticism and argument that forced me to think more deeply.

Most of all, I owe an unpayably large debt to my wife, Sue. She served as an exceptionally able critic; more, she is my unshakable friend and companion.

Contents

Introduction

I WRITE THIS INTRODUCTION in late fall of 2005 thinking back seventeen years to 1988 when, as a young man, I was hard at work on *The End of Nature*. It was the first book for a general audience about global warming; there were details then that no one yet knew. But—sadly—the story has played out as I expected at the time. By now, everyone knows more or less what's going on. Still, it's astounding to watch how deep and relentless the change has been. On this morning, for instance, Hurricane Wilma, the record-setting twenty-first named storm of the year, bears down on the Gulf of Mexico. The pressure in its center this morning was the lowest ever recorded in the Atlantic. It follows by a few weeks the unmatched destruction of Katrina—and by a few more weeks a paper in *Nature* demonstrating that on average hurricanes now last 60 percent longer and have peak winds 50 percent greater than a generation earlier.

Meanwhile, here are a few of the other developments on planet Earth in the last ten weeks:

• The scientists tracking Arctic sea ice reported that for the fourth year in a row it was diminishing, and at an accelerating pace— an area twice the size of Texas had vanished. As that melt progressed, it triggered its own feedback effect: instead of white ice to bounce the sun's rays back out to space, blue water now absorbed that solar energy, amplifying the process. "We may have reached a tipping point," one researcher said.

• A British team released a new study of soils, showing that as the planet has warmed and the period between frosts lengthened (winter is now eleven days shorter on average than in 1970), microbial activity in the top layers of the ground is increasing. This decay is in turn releasing carbon stored in the soil, again amplifying the greenhouse effect. And not by a trivial amount: The thirteen million tons of carbon released annually in the British Isles is enough to completely offset all the fairly ambitious work the British have done to change their energy practices in the last two decades.

• Similarly, researchers in Russia's far north recently released data showing that the permafrost beneath the tundra is melting at record rates, and in the process releasing quantities of methane, another potent greenhouse gas. In fact, last winter so much methane was suddenly perking out to the surface that in places the bubbling kept open water from freezing.

In the late 1980s, we didn't completely understand the sensitivity of the earth's physical systems to small shifts in temperature. Most of the scientists I talked to then would not have predicted that a 1-degree rise in global average temperature—which is what we have so far caused—would be enough to so thoroughly disrupt the planet. But it has. The world is a different place—more chaotic, storm tossed, disease ridden. Here's one way of saying it: in 1968, when I was a boy, Apollo 8 sent back the first pictures of our planet, that blue-white marble floating in space. Well, those pictures are as out of date as my high school yearbook photo. The planet doesn't look like that or behave like that anymore—there's more blue and less white, more cyclones swirling in the tropics. It's a different Earth; we might as well hold a contest to pick a new name.

We also have a far better idea of what's ahead than we did in 1989. The ever more finely calibrated computer models converge on a forecast of about 5 degrees additional warming in the course of this century unless we make heroic efforts to wean ourselves from fossil fuels. If that happens, the planet will be warmer than it's been in at least thirty million years. Not warmer than it's been in human history. Warmer than it's been since before the beginning of primate evolution.

We begin to sense more clearly now what that might mean. Just to give one small example: Hurricane Katrina created a million refugees. Scientists using various computer models have calculated that there may be 150 million such refugees by mid-century—that is, 150 simultaneous Katrinas, most of them in the poorest parts of the low-lying tropics. And the computer models also hint at surprises lurking ahead—thresholds over which the world might trip as it warms so rapidly. For instance, all that melting Arctic ice could conceivably dilute the North Atlantic enough to slow or even stop the Gulf Stream.

Such forecasts should not distract from the immediate message: Global warming is not a problem for the future. It is here now, each year emerging with more power, each year closer to assuming its destiny as the most important fact in our politics, economies, and daily lives. That sense of imminence is new.

But if the cycles of the Earth now move more quickly—spring on average comes *a week earlier* across the Northern Hemisphere than it did just two decades ago—human society seems, at least on this most important of issues, to be paralyzed. Political and economic time has stood still for a decade: despite a few international conferences and grand declarations, we've done next to nothing to stem the flow of carbon dioxide that fuels global warming. In fact, the United States alone now pours nearly 15 percent more CO_2 into the atmosphere than it did when this book was first published. In 1989, I said we needed to drive smaller cars and drive them less; in the intervening years, average Americans took to piloting vehicles that would turn General Patton green with envy. We're not getting it.

It is the contrast between the pace at which the physical world is changing and the pace at which the human society is reacting that constitutes the key environmental fact of our time.

SEVENTEEN YEARS AGO, those of us who were convinced that the climate was warming fast were out on a limb. A sturdy limb—the fact that carbon dioxide trapped heat near the planet seemed irrefutable—but a limb nonetheless. All the studies and reports that cataloged the greenhouse effect fit neatly on my desk when I was writing this book; the science was still, in many ways, rudimentary. And so it was no surprise when that science, and the conclusions drawn from it, came under attack. That's how science works—each hypothesis tortured to find its weakness. By now, the studies on global warming would fill an airplane hangar. Postdocs have tapped into tundra, overflown rain forests, launched satellites, collected ancient pollen, counted tree rings, cored ice sheets, floated weather balloons, sent sound waves across entire oceans. Unlike the politicians, they really have worked overtime. And what have they learned? That the predictions of a decade ago were remarkably close to correct. We know a lot more about cloud formation and sulfur particles and sunspots than we did in 1989, but the expectation about how it will all sum out is essentially the same—human beings, with their cars and factories and burning rain forests, will increase the planet's temperature 3 or 4 degrees in the century to come.

Accidents of one kind or another helped speed the scientific work. Most notably, when Mount Pinatubo in the Philippines erupted with spectacular force in 1992, it filled the sky with an easily estimated quantity of various chemicals. The scientists running the various computer models of the planet's climate could plug those estimates right into their programs and forecast what would happen in the years ahead. NASA's James Hansen, who had already done more than anyone else to warn the world about the greenhouse effect, made the gutsiest call, issuing a precise prediction for how the planet's temperature would shift, month by month, in the next three years. At first he seemed to have missed, and greenhouse skeptics jumped all over the early results, using them to call the whole theory into question. But at a memorable scientific meeting in Hawaii, Hansen stood up and said, "I believe this is one case where the model is right and the world is wrong." And indeed, beginning with the very next month's readings, global temperatures began to match his predictions with eerie precision. The incident was one of many that made climatologists more confident of their complex models, and by 1995 the scientific jury had delivered its verdict. The International Panel on Climate Change, a collection of 1,500 scientists assembled by the United Nations, summarized all the data and concluded with this dry but historic understatement: "The balance of evidence suggests that there is a discernible human influence on global climate." The same panel, in 2001, hardened their language and toughened their forecast.

In other words, global warming no longer belonged in the category of distant and speculative threats. It was not like the danger of an asteroid strike. Instead, it was *under way*—we were in the rapids, not the smooth water above them. And, in fact, researchers increasingly insisted that they could see its effects, even in these relatively early stages. As the air warms, it should evaporate more water from the surface, and it should then drop that extra water back on the planet—in other words, there should be an increase both in drought and in rainfall. One would expect events like the forest fires that turned day into night across Malaysia and Indonesia in 1997, or like the flooding that struck China, Bangladesh, Korea, Mexico, and a dozen other places in 1998. A study reported two years ago by Thomas Karl of the National Oceanic and Atmospheric Administration showed that "extreme precipitation events"—those storms that dump more than two inches of water in twenty-four hours—had increased 20 percent across our continent compared with 1900. That's an almost unbelievable surge. "If you look out your window, part of what you see in terms of weather is produced by ourselves," says Karl. "If you look out the window fifty years from now, we're going to be responsible for more of it."

But the message of the rainfall and the ice melt, and the dramatic findings of the scientific community, has been muted, thanks to a powerful campaign of disinformation launched and funded by those industries that can't imagine a future without fossil fuels.

In the past year, for instance, the most widely read account of global warming came from the novelist Michael Crichton, who argued it was all a ridiculous panic engineered by environmental groups to speed fund-raising. When the relevant Senate committee (chaired by Oklahoma's James Inhofe, who has called climate change history's "greatest hoax") convened to take testimony this fall, they didn't summon the hurricane scientists, or the soil scientists, or the ice scientists. They asked for . . . Crichton.

The tiny squad of climate-change skeptics, backed by lots of coal and oil money, never let up. Any tiny caveat in the deluge of studies—some scientist's admission that the computer forecasts are by their very nature "uncertain"—is seized upon as conclusive proof that the whole greenhouse theory is a sham. In 1998, during the warmest year in our history to that point, a huge petition emerged, supposedly signed by thousands of scientists who think global warming won't occur; after widespread coverage, it turned out to be a worthless compilation of undocumented names collected over the Internet, including such luminaries as the Spice Girls.

I repeat—seventeen years ago such reactions were not only to be expected, they were necessary. It was part of the process; if journalists had not sought balance from the competing scientific camps, they would not have been doing their jobs. But by now it is an intellectual fraud to continue spreading the notion that global warming is one more theory that may or may not prove true.

THE SCIENCE, however, was only one part of the original book—and not its most important. What mattered most to me was the inference I drew from that science: that for the first time human beings had become so large that they altered everything around us. That we had ended nature as an independent force, that our appetites and habits and desires could now be read in every cubic meter of air, in every increment on the thermometer.

This doesn't make the consequences of global warming any worse in a practical sense, of course—we'd be in as tough a spot if the temperature was going up for entirely "natural" reasons. But to me it made this historical moment entirely different from any other, filled with implications for our philosophy, our theology, our sense of self. We are no longer able to think of ourselves as a species tossed about by larger forces—now we *are* those larger forces. Hurricanes and thunderstorms and tornadoes become not acts of God but acts of man. That was what I meant by the "end of nature."

Of course, everyone thinks they live at the hinge points of history. The academic debate that followed the book's release was, and continues to be, lively; many critics claimed that we weren't really "ending" nature because either we had been altering our surroundings for centuries, or we were a part of nature ourselves and hence couldn't destroy it.

Both objections, of course, are true. Emerging into the world hairless, slow, and relatively weak, we've had to use our one asset—our largish brains—to alter our surroundings. We've changed the places where we lived, the places where we grew our food, and even to some extent the wildernesses surrounding them. On this continent, for instance, the Indians would periodically burn sections of forest and prairie to improve the hunting. But always before, our disruptions had some boundary to them; they were akin to the work of the beaver who lives next to me and manages to flood quite a large section of the lowland behind his dam. But there are plenty of places beyond the reach of his high water. Similarly, you could always find vast territory where human influence mattered not at all.

Beginning with the invisible releases of radiation, and then the toxic pollutants like DDT, and then the by-products of large-scale industrialization like acid rain, though, we began to alter even those places where we were not. Short of wide-scale nuclear war, global warming represents the largest imaginable such alteration: by changing the very temperature of the planet, we inexorably affect its flora, its fauna, its rainfall and evaporation, the decomposition of its soils. Every inch of the planet is different; indeed, the physics of climate means the most extreme changes are going on at the North and South poles, farthest from human beings. The by-products—the pollutants—of one species have become the most powerful force for change on the planet. This change in quantity is so large that it becomes a change in quality. The story of our moment, of these few short decades when we happen to be alive, is the story of crossing that threshold.

And of course it is also true that we are part of nature—indeed, over the last few centuries we've forgotten, to our peril, how connected we actually are to the rest of the fabric of creation. But to me this does not make our blundering alteration of everything around us any more defensible or any less sad. Imagine that you have hiked to the edge of a pond in the forest and stand there admiring the sunset. If you should happen to look down and see a Coke can that someone has tossed there in the rushes, it will affect you differently than if you see a pile of deer droppings. And the reason, or at least one reason, is our intuitive understanding that the person who dropped the Coke can didn't need to, any more than we need to go on raising the temperature of the planet. We *are* different from the rest of the natural order, for the single reason that we possess the possibility of self-restraint, of choosing some other way.

WHICH BRINGS US around again to politics, to the realm where we will make the collective decision on whether or not to restrain ourselves. Seventeen years ago, I said I thought real change would be extremely difficult, because addressing the issue meant altering the fundamentals of our lives. In important ways, modern human beings are machines for burning fossil fuels. Therefore, to level off fossil fuel consumption, much less reduce it the 70 percent the scientists say is necessary, involves tinkering with virtually every facet of our daily lives. We would need to change the ways we move ourselves around, the spaces we live in, the jobs we perform, the food we eat.

It's not that it *can't* be done. I've spent much of the past two decades looking for ways out, for places that work. In a book called *Hope, Human and Wild*, I've written about the city of Curitiba, in Brazil, where the bus system is so marvelous that its citizens use a third less fuel than other Brazilians. I've spent time in the Indian state of Kerala, where, on an annual income of $300 and hence with minimal environmental impact on the globe, people have life expectancies, birthrates, and literacy rates that rival our own.

But such examples run completely counter to the trend of the past two decades. In 1989, when I wrote *The End of Nature*, we still fretted about what would happen to the environment *if* China became a consumer nation. I spent the summer just past in China, reporting on that country's full emergence as an economic superpower. Now, we watch as they add the equivalent of Southern California's generating capacity to their electric grid each year, almost all of it powered by coal. Not that China is the villain here—they are using that fossil fuel as we did a century ago, to pull people out of poverty. And their growth really underscores the staggering size of our own addiction—the average Chinese still only uses one-ninth as much energy as the average American. With the Cold War long since over, the most powerful ideology by far is consumerism—there is no place on the planet that does not fall under the enchantment of our images of the good life.

In some ways, the most dismal development of the last seventeen years—even more than the ever-darkening science—is the inability of the American political system to take seriously our peril. Nothing fundamental has shifted in our scientific understanding since 1988—as this book makes clear by its mere existence, we knew enough long ago to get to work, and if we had, our peril would be smaller. But we didn't. A bipartisan effort to do nothing has been wildly successful. The Clinton-Gore administration oversaw the conversion of the American vehicle fleet from cars to semimilitary vehicles, and a resulting 15 percent increase in carbon emissions. George W. Bush renounced the Kyoto treaty within a few weeks of taking office, beginning the downfall of our public image around the world that has continued unabated. His administration's energy plan foresees a future where we drill, mine, refine, and combust our way to 30 percent more carbon emissions within a generation.

This is particularly sad since in other ways an alternative future path is easier to envision than it was in 1989. Then, environmentalists talked about alternative energy with their fingers crossed: solar power was for noble aging hippies who wanted to mess around in their basements with an array of batteries. Now, the panels on my roof in the mountains of the Northeast tie directly into the grid. When the sun is out, I become a utility, with the pleasure of watching my electric meter spin backward. Wind power, though still a small source of power, is the fastest-growing means of electricity generation around the world. My hybrid Honda Civic gets me fifty-seven miles to the gallon.

So far, though, neither the new technologies nor the new crises seem to be spurring much demand for change.

One reason may be the intuitive sense that in some ways it's too late to do anything about it all—that the physical forces we've unleashed are so large and terrifying that raising the gas tax a dime or even a dollar seems almost comically puny in comparison. In a way, this intuition is completely correct: it's far too late to stop global warming. All we can do is make it less bad than it will otherwise be. Our crusade, if we ever mount it, will be on behalf of a relatively livable world, not on behalf of the world that we were born into.

THE SCARIEST PART of the chemistry of global warming involves "feedback loops"—the idea that as you raise the temperature you cause changes that will raise the temperature even more. If you warm the Arctic, for instance, thawing tundra may release huge amounts of carbon that will in turn accelerate the warming.

But in ending nature, in finishing off that separate realm that has always served to make us feel smaller, we've completed a feedback loop of our own. It's harder to go to the forest now, or to the mountains, or to the ocean, or even to a patch of wildflowers and feel the same kind of wonderful smallness. Those Coke cans are everywhere. We're everywhere.

I have had the great luxury of living in the Adirondack Mountains of upstate New York and the Green Mountains of Vermont these past two decades—one of the few regions on the planet that gets more wild with each passing season. Thanks to the wisdom of the people of New York, the Adirondacks is a vast protected wilderness, one where people live in and among the rest of creation. You can still feel small here sometimes, which is for me the great antidote to despair. My daughter, now thirteen years old, has grown up with an abiding sense of nature's size and peace and meaning. But even its untouched wildernesses are threatened by climate change and by the myriad of other human excesses. Its winters grow shorter, it summers hotter, its forests less stable. In the past decade, a great windstorm and an epic ice storm have passed through here, leveling thousands of square miles of forest. By the old way of reckoning, these were not disasters, just extreme incidences of the powerful forces that made this place. But now who knows what mixture of "nature" and of "us" they embody? Who knows what they mean?

So people sometimes ask: How should I cope with the sadness of watching nature end in our lifetimes, and with the guilt of knowing that each of us is in some measure responsible? The answer to the second part is easier: at the very least, we have to put up a good fight. I've worked on and written about materialism, population, and planning in the last decade, knowing that how well we control our numbers, our appetites, and the efficiency with which we satisfy those appetites will ordain just how desperate the situation becomes. They are the battles for our time, as morally compulsory as the battles for civil rights or against totalitarianism.

But even with that work, the sadness that drove me to write this book in the first place has not really lifted. This home of ours, the blessed hunk of rock and sky and biology that we were born onto, becomes each day a less complex and a more violent place; its rhythms of season and storm shifted and shattered. We didn't create this world, but we are busy decreating it. Still the sun rises; still the moon wanes and waxes; but they look down on a planet that means something different than it used to. Something less than it used to. This buzzing, blooming, mysterious, cruel, lovely globe of mountain, sea, city, forest; of fish and wolf and bug and man; of carbon and hydrogen and nitrogen—it has come unbalanced in our short moment on it. It's mostly us now.

And since it's mostly us, we better finally think about who the hell we are. In 1989, with the solipsism of someone in his midtwenties, I focused on individual human efforts—smaller families, reduced consumption, and so on. I still think these are important, but I've come to think that equally important changes lie elsewhere: in the direction of stronger, tighter communities.

To understand why, consider one set of statistics: the average western European uses about half as much energy as the average American. This is not because they're living austere lives or dwelling in caves: as travelers know, life in Paris or Amsterdam or Oslo is as elegant and dignified as anything America has to offer. Nor is it because they possess some miracle technology. Instead it's because they order their lives differently, placing less emphasis on the individual and more on the community. Hence, their taxes support vibrant cities that attract citizens instead of repelling them into the surrounding suburban sprawl. Hence, they are willing to use public transit instead of insisting on taking their own vehicles everywhere they go. And so on. That 50 percent is a big number. It offers some hope—if we can head in that direction, and get the Chinese and the Indians pointed there too, then perhaps climate change can be kept from spinning completely out of control. But it won't be easy. Perhaps the most important summation of American thinking came a couple of years after I wrote *The End of Nature*. The elder President Bush was facing a reelection battle against Bill Clinton, and so advisers persuaded him to attend the world environmental summit in Rio de Janeiro, possibly the most optimistic moment in recent history. Before he went, however, he told a press conference that "the American way of life is not up for negotiation." If that's true, if we can't imagine living any differently, then all else is mere commentary.

Our recalcitrance won't last forever, of course. Sooner or later events will break through even our carefully buttressed denial. (This fall has seen a spike in gas prices, and that's been enough to break our love affair with SUVs. But if higher oil prices also lead us to increase our use of coal, in the long run it will hurt, not help, our global warming efforts.) That breakthrough, however, needs to come sooner rather than later. The science has grown steadily more alarming in the last seventeen years—some of the data outlined in the pages that follow has been superseded, but in every case by even scarier numbers. And now the planet is starting to warp in the way that researchers predicted. Time grows short; the need grows desperate. People ask me sometimes if I would change anything in this book were I to write it again. And of course I would—there are passages that are the work of a much younger man. Some of them make me wince. But the only thing I would really change, if I could, are the facts. I've spent every day since its publication praying that this book would be proved wrong. Those prayers have not been answered.

Part I

THE PRESENT

A New Atmosphere

NATURE, WE BELIEVE, takes forever. It moves with infinite slowness through the many periods of its history, whose names we dimly recall from high school biology—the Devonian, the Triassic, the Cretaceous, the Pleistocene. Ever since Darwin, nature writers have taken pains to stress the incomprehensible length of this path. "So slowly, oh, so slowly have the great changes been brought about," wrote John Burroughs at the turn of the century. "The Orientals try to get a hint of eternity by saying that when the Himalayas have been ground to powder by allowing a gauze veil to float against them once in a thousand years, eternity will only just have begun. Our mountains have been pulverized by a process almost as slow." We have been told that man's tenure is as a minute to the earth's day, but it is that vast day which has lodged in our minds. The age of the trilobites began some 600 million years ago. The dinosaurs lived for nearly 140 million years. Since even a million years is utterly unfathomable, the message is: Nothing happens quickly. Change takes unimaginable—"geologic"—time.

This idea about time is essentially mistaken. Muddled though they are scientifically, the creationists, believing in the sudden appearance of the earth some seven thousand years ago, may intuitively understand more about the progress of time than the rest of us. For the world as we know it—that is, the world with human beings formed into some sort of civilization, the world in which North America, Europe, and much of the rest of the planet are warm enough to support large human populations—is of quite comprehensible duration. People began to collect in a rudimentary society in the north of Mesopotamia some ten or twelve thousand years ago. Using thirty years as a generation, that is three hundred and thirty to four hundred generations ago. Sitting here at my desk, I can think back five generations in my family—I have seen photos of four. That is, I can think back nearly one-sixtieth of the way to the start of civilization. A skilled genealogist might get me one-thirtieth of the distance back. And I can conceive of how most of those forebears lived. From the work of archaeologists and from accounts like those in the Bible I have some sense of daily life at least as far back as the time of the pharaohs, which is more than a third of the way. Two hundred and sixty-five generations ago Jericho was a walled city of three thousand souls. Two hundred and sixty-five is a large number, but not in the way that six hundred million is a large number—not inscrutably large.

Or look at it this way: There are plants on this earth as old as civilization. Not species—individual plants. The General Sherman tree in California's Sequoia National Park may be a third as old, about four thousand years. Certain Antarctic lichens date back ten thousand years. A specific creosote plant in the southwestern desert was estimated recently to be 11,700 years of age.

And within that ten or twelve thousand years of civilization, of course, time is not uniform. The world as we really know it dates back perhaps to the Renaissance. The world as we really, *really* know it dates back to the Industrial Revolution. The world we actually feel comfortable in dates back to perhaps 1945. It was not until after World War II, for instance, that plastics came into widespread use.

In other words, our reassuring sense of a timeless future, which is drawn from that apparently bottomless well of the past, is a delusion. True, evolution, grinding on ever so slowly, has taken billions of years to create us from slime, but that does not mean that time always moves so ponderously. Events, enormous events, can happen quickly. We've known this to be true since Hiroshima, of course, but I don't mean *that* quickly. I mean that over a year or a decade or a lifetime big and impersonal and dramatic changes can take place. We're now comfortable with the bizarre idea that continents can drift over eons, or that continents can die in an atomic second; even so, normal time seems to us immune from such huge changes. It isn't, though. In the last three decades, for example, the amount of carbon dioxide in the atmosphere has increased more than 10 percent, from about 315 to more than 350 parts per million. In the last decade, an immense "hole" in the ozone layer has opened above the South Pole. In the last half-decade, the percentage of West German forests damaged by acid rain has risen from less than 10 to more than 50. According to the Worldwatch Institute, in 1988—for the first time since that starved Pilgrim—America ate more food than it grew. Burroughs again: "One summer day, while I was walking along the country road on the farm where I was born, a section of the stone wall opposite me, and not more than three or four yards distant, suddenly fell down. Amid the general stillness and immobility about me the effect was quite startling. . . . It was the sudden summing up of half a century or more of atomic changes in the material of the wall. A grain or two of sand yielded to the pressure of long years, and gravity did the rest."

In much the same comforting way that we think of time as imponderably long, we consider the earth to be inconceivably large. Although with the advent of spaceflight it became fashionable to picture the planet as a small orb of life and light in a dark, cold vastness, that image never really sank in. To any one of us, the earth *is* enormous, "infinite to our senses." Or, at least, it is if we think about it in the usual horizontal dimensions: even the frequent flier with the most bonus miles has seen only a tiny fraction of the earth's terrain; even the most intrepid mariner cuts a single furrow across the ocean field. There are vast spaces between my house, in the Adirondack Mountains of upstate New York, and Manhattan—it's a five-hour drive through one state in one country of one continent. But from my house to the post office at the end of the road is a trip of six and a half miles. On a bicycle it takes about twenty-five minutes, in a car eight or nine. I've walked it in an hour and a half. If you turned that trip on its end, the twenty-five-minute pedal past

Bateman's sandpit and the graveyard and the waterfall and Allen Hill would take me a mile beyond the height of Mt. Everest, past the point where the air is too thin to breathe without artificial assistance. Into that tight space, and the layer of ozone just above it, is crammed all that is life and all that maintains life.

This, I realize, is a far from novel observation. I repeat it only to make the same case I made with regard to time. The world is not so large as we intuitively believe—space can be as short as time. For instance, the average American car driven the average American distance—ten thousand miles—in an average American year releases its own weight in carbon into the atmosphere. Imagine each car on a busy freeway pumping a ton of carbon into the atmosphere, and the sky seems less infinitely blue.

Along with our optimistic perceptions of time and space, some comparatively minor misunderstandings distort our sense of the world. Consider the American failure to convert to the metric system. Like all schoolchildren of my vintage, I spent many days listening to teachers explain liters and meters and hectares and all the other logical units of measurement, and promptly forgot it all. We all did, except those of us who became scientists, who always use such units. As a result, if I read there will be an 0.8-degree Celsius rise in the temperature between now and the year 2000, it sounds less ominous than a degree and a half Fahrenheit. Similarly, a ninety-centimeter rise in sea level sounds less ominous than a one-yard rise; and neither of them sounds so ominous until one stops to think that over a beach with a normal slope such a rise would bring the ocean ninety meters (that's 295 feet) above its current tide line. In somewhat the same way, the logarithmic scale that we use to determine the overall composition of our soils or waters—pH—distorts reality like a fun-house mirror for anyone who doesn't use it on a daily basis. For instance, "normal" rainwater has a pH of 5.6. But the acidified rain that falls on the Adirondacks has a pH between 4.6 and 4.2—that is, it is ten to fourteen times as acid.

Of all such quirks, though, the most ephemeral may be the most significant. It is an accident of the calendar: we live too close to the year 2000. Forever we have read about the year 2000. It has become a symbol of the bright and distant future, when we will ride in air cars and talk on video phones. The year 2010 still sounds far off, almost unreachably far off, as though it were on the other side of a great body of water. If someone says to me that a very bad thing will happen in 2010, I may feign concern but subconsciously I file it away. So it always shocks me when I realize that 2010 is almost as close as 1970—closer than the breakup of the Beatles—and that the turn of the century is no further in front of us than Ronald Reagan's election to the presidency is behind. We live in the shadow of a number, and that makes it hard for us to see the future.

Our comforting sense of the permanence of our natural world, our confidence that it will change gradually and imperceptibly if at all, is, then, the result of a subtly warped perspective. Changes that can affect us can happen in our lifetime in our world—not just changes like wars but bigger and more sweeping events. I believe that without recognizing it we have already stepped over the threshold of such a change: that we are at the end of nature.

By the end of nature I do not mean the end of the world. The rain will still fall and the sun shine, though differently than before. When I say "nature," I mean a certain set of human ideas about the world and our place in it. But the death of those ideas begins with concrete changes in the reality around us—changes that scientists can measure and enumerate. More and more frequently, these changes will clash with our perceptions, until, finally, our sense of nature as eternal and separate is washed away, and we will see all too clearly what we have done.

SVANTE ARRHENIUS took his doctorate in physics at the University of Uppsala in 1884. His thesis earned him the lowest possible grade short of outright refusal. Nineteen years later that thesis, which was on the conductivity of solutions, earned him the Nobel Prize. He subsequently accounted for the initial poor reception this way: "I came to my professor, Cleve, whom I admired very much, and I said, 'I have a new theory of electrical conductivity as a cause of chemical reactions.' He said, 'This is very interesting,' and then he said, 'Goodbye.' He explained to me later that he knew very well that there are so many different theories formed, and that they are almost certain to be wrong, for after a short time they disappeared; and therefore, by using the statistical manner of forming his ideas, he concluded that my theory also would not exist long."

Arrhenius's understanding of electrolytic conduction was not his only shrug-provoking new idea. As he surveyed the first few decades of the Industrial Revolution he realized that man was burning coal at an unprecedented rate, "evaporating our coal mines into the air." Scientists already knew that carbon dioxide, a by-product of fossil fuel combustion, trapped infrared radiation that would otherwise have reflected back out to space. Jean-Baptiste Joseph Fourier, who developed the theory of heat conduction (and who was also one of the earliest students of Egyptian archaeology), had speculated about the effect nearly a century before, and, indeed, had even used the hothouse as a metaphor. But it was Arrhenius who, employing measurements of infrared radiation from the full moon, did the first calculations of the possible effects of man's stepped-up production of carbon dioxide. The average global temperature, he concluded, would rise as much as 9 degrees if the amount of carbon dioxide in the air doubled from its preindustrial level. That is, heat waves in mid-American latitudes would run into the 110s, the 120s, the 130s; the seas would rise many feet; crops would wither in the fields.

This idea floated in obscurity for a very long time. Now and then a few scientists took it up—the British physicist G. S. Callendar speculated in the 1930s, for instance, that increasing carbon dioxide levels could account for a warming of North America and northern Europe that meteorologists had begun to observe in the 1880s. But that warming seemed to be replaced by a temperature decline around 1940; anyway, most scientists were too busy creating better living through petroleum to be bothered with such long-term speculation. And those few who did consider the problem concluded that the oceans, which hold much more carbon dioxide than the atmosphere, would soak up any excess that man churned out—that the oceans were an infinite sink down which to pour the problem.

Then, in 1957, two scientists at California's Scripps Institution of Oceanography, Roger Revelle and Hans Suess, published a paper in the journal *Tellus* on this matter of the oceans. What they found was dismaying. No, more than dismaying—what they found may turn out to be the single most important limit in an age of limits, the central awkward fact of a hot and constrained planet.

What they found was that the conventional wisdom was wrong: the upper layer of the oceans, where air and sea meet and transact their business, would absorb very little of the excess carbon dioxide produced by man.

To be precise, what they demonstrated was that "a rather small change in the amount of free carbon dioxide dissolved in seawater corresponds to a relatively large change in the pressure of carbon dioxide at which the oceans and the atmosphere are at equilibrium." To be dramatic, what they showed was that most of the carbon dioxide being pumped into the air by millions of smokestacks, furnaces, and car exhausts would stay in the air, where, presumably, it would gradually warm the planet. "Human beings are now carrying out a large-scale geophysical experiment of a kind that could not have happened in the past, nor be repeated in the future," they wrote. This experiment, they added with the morbid understatement of true scientists, "if adequately documented, may yield a far-reaching insight into the processes determining weather and climate."

While there are other parts to this story—the depletion of the ozone, acid rain, genetic engineering—the story of the end of nature really begins with that greenhouse experiment, with what will happen to the weather.

WHEN WE DRILL into an oil field, we tap into a vast reservoir of organic matter that has been in storage for millennia. We unbury it. When we burn that oil (or coal or natural gas) we release its carbon into the atmosphere in the form of carbon dioxide. This is not pollution in the normal sense of the word. Carbon *monoxide* is "pollution," an unnecessary by-product. A clean-burning engine releases less of it. But when it comes to carbon dioxide, a clean-burning engine is no better than the motor on a Model T. It will emit about 5.6 pounds of carbon in the form of carbon dioxide for every gallon of gasoline it consumes. In the course of about a hundred years, our various engines and fires have released a substantial amount of the carbon that has been buried over time. It is as if someone had scrimped and saved his entire life, and then spent every cent on one fantastic week's debauch. In this, if nothing else, wrote the great biologist A. J. Lotka, "the present is an eminently atypical epoch." We are living on our capital, as we began to realize during the gas crises of the 1970s. But it is more than waste, more than a binge. We are spending that capital in such a way as to alter the atmosphere. It is like taking that week's fling and, in the process, contracting a horrid disease.

There has always been, at least since the start of life, a certain amount of carbon dioxide in the atmosphere, and it has always trapped a certain amount of sunlight to warm the earth. If there were no carbon dioxide, our world might resemble Mars—it would probably be so cold as to be lifeless. A little bit of greenhouse is a good thing, then—the plant that is life thrives in its warmth. The question is: How much? On Venus the atmosphere is 97 percent carbon dioxide. As a result, it traps infrared radiation a hundred times more efficiently than the earth's atmosphere, and keeps the planet a toasty 700 degrees warmer than the earth. The earth's atmosphere is mostly nitrogen and oxygen; there's currently only about .035 percent carbon dioxide, hardly more than a trace. The worries about the greenhouse effect are actually worries about raising that figure from .035 percent to .055 or .06 percent, which is not very much. But plenty, it turns out, to make everything different.

In 1957, when Revelle and Suess wrote their paper, no one even knew for certain that carbon dioxide was increasing. The Scripps Institution hired a young scientist, Charles Keeling, and he set up monitoring stations at the South Pole and 11,150 feet above the Pacific on the side of Mauna Loa in Hawaii. His readings soon confirmed the Revelle-Suess hypothesis: the atmosphere was filling with carbon dioxide. When Keeling took his first readings in 1958, the atmosphere at Mauna Loa contained about 315 parts per million of carbon dioxide. Subsequent readings showed that each year the figure increased, and at a growing rate. Initially the annual increase was about .7 parts per million; now it is at least twice that, or 1.5 parts per million. Admittedly, 1.5 parts per million sounds absurdly small. But by drilling holes into glaciers and testing the air trapped in ancient ice, even by looking at the air sealed in old telescopes, scientists have calculated that the atmosphere prior to the Industrial Revolution contained about 280 parts per million carbon dioxide, and, in fact, that that was as high a level as had been recorded in the past 160,000 years. The current reading is near 360 parts per million. At a rate of 1.5 parts per million per year, pre–Industrial Revolution concentration of carbon dioxide in the atmosphere would be doubled in the next 140 years. And since, as we have seen, carbon dioxide at a very low level helps determine the climate, carbon dioxide at double that very low level, even if it's still small in absolute terms, could have enormous effect. It's like misreading a recipe and baking bread for two hours instead of one: it matters.

But the 1.5 parts per million annual increase is not a given; it seems nearly certain to go higher. The essential facts here are demographic and economic, not chemical. The world's population has more than tripled in this century and, according to UN statistics released in May of 1989, is expected to double and perhaps nearly triple again before reaching a plateau in the next century. (At the moment, after a decade or two of improving, the trends may be getting worse—China's fertility rate increased from 2.1 to 2.4 children per woman in 1986 and has remained there since.) And the tripled population has not contented itself with using only three times the resources. In the last century industrial production has grown fiftyfold. Four-fifths of that growth has come since 1950, and almost all of it, of course, has been based on fossil fuels. And in the next half century, the United Nations predicts, this $13 trillion economy will grow another five to ten times larger.

These physical facts are almost as stubborn as the chemistry of infrared absorption. They mean that the world will use more energy—between 2 and 3 percent more each year by most estimates. And the largest increases may come in the use of coal. That is bad news, since coal spews more carbon dioxide into the atmo-sphere than any other sort of energy (twice as much as natural gas, for instance). China, which has the world's largest coal reserves and recently surpassed the Soviet Union as the world's largest coal pro-ducer, has plans to almost double her coal consumption by the year 2000.

In other words, this is not something that has been happening for a long time. It is not a marathon or the twenty-four hours of Le Mans. It's a hundred-yard dash, a drag race, getting faster all the time. If energy use and other contributions to carbon dioxide levels continue to grow exponentially, a model devised by the World Re-sources Institute predicts that carbon dioxide levels prior to the In-dustrial Revolution will have doubled by about 2040; if they grow somewhat more slowly, as most estimates predict, the level would double sometime around 2070. The leaders of the seven major in-dustrial democracies agreed at their summit in mid-July 1989 to "strongly advocate common efforts" to limit carbon dioxide, but nothing more, in part because the solutions are neither obvious nor easy. For example, installing some sort of scrubber on a power-plant smokestack to get rid of the carbon dioxide would seem an obvious fix. But a system that removed 90 percent of the carbon dioxide would also reduce the effective capacity of the plant 80 percent. One oft-heard suggestion is to use more nuclear power. But because so much of our energy use is for things like automobile fuel, even if we mustered the political will and economic resources to quickly replace every single electric generating station with a nuclear power plant, our total carbon dioxide output would fall little more than a quarter. Ditto, at least initially, for cold fusion or hot fusion or any other clean method of producing energy. So the sacrifices de-manded may be on a scale we can't imagine and won't like.

BURNING FOSSIL FUELS is not the only method human beings have devised to increase the level of atmospheric carbon dioxide. Burning down a forest also sends clouds of carbon into the air. Trees and shrubby forests still cover 40 percent of the land on earth, but this area has shrunk by about a third since preagricultural times, and that shrinkage, it almost goes without saying, is accelerating. In the Brazilian state of Pará, for instance, 180,000 square kilometers was deforested between 1975 and 1986; in the hundred years preceding that decade, settlers had hacked away about 18,000 square kilometers. "At night, roaring and red, the forest looks to be at war," one correspondent wrote. The Brazilian government has tried to slow down the burning, but it employs only nine hundred forest wardens for an area larger than Europe.

This is not news—it's well known that the rain forests are disappearing, and are taking with them most of the world's plant and animal species. But forget for a moment that we are losing a unique resource, a cradle of life, irreplaceable grandeur, and so forth. The dense, layered rain forest contains three to five times more carbon per acre than an open, dry forest: an acre of Brazil up in flames equals three to five acres of Yellowstone. Deforestation currently adds between 1 billion and 2.5 billion tons of carbon to the atmosphere annually, 20 percent or more of the amount produced by fossil fuel burning. And that acre of rain forest, which has poor soil and can support crops for only a few years, soon turns to desert, or, at least, to pastureland.

And where there's pasture there are cows, and what cows support in their intestines are huge numbers of anaerobic bacteria, which break down the cellulose that cows chew. That is why cows, unlike people, can eat grass. Why does this matter? Because those bugs that digest the cellulose excrete methane. Methane, or natural gas, gives off carbon dioxide when burned, though only half as much as oil. When it escapes into the atmosphere *without* being burned, though, it is twenty times more efficient than carbon dioxide at trapping solar radiation and warming the planet. So even though it makes up less than two parts per million of the atmosphere, it can have a significant effect. Even though much of the methane in the atmosphere comes from seemingly "natural" sources—the methanogenic bacteria—their present huge numbers are clearly man made. Mankind owns 1.2 billion head of cattle, not to mention a large number of camels, horses, pigs, sheep, and goats, and together they belch about 73 million metric tons of methane into the air each year, a 435 percent increase in the last century. The buffalo and wildebeest they displaced belched as well, but their numbers were not as great.

We have raised the number of termites, too, and still more dramatically. Termites have the same bacteria in their intestines as cows; that is why they can digest wood. We tend to think of termites as house wreckers, but in most of the world they are house builders, erecting elaborate, rock-hard mounds twenty or thirty feet high. Inside these fortresses an elaborate hierarchy of termites guards the queens—some of the termites sport sharp pincers longer than their bodies; others have heads shaped like drain plugs, so they can block up the interior passages against intruders; still others explode when attacked, or squirt poison. If a bulldozer razes a mound, worker termites can rebuild it in hours. They are like most animals in that their numbers are limited only by the supply of food. And when we hack down a rain forest, all of a sudden there's dead wood everywhere—food galore. Termites have a "high digestion efficiency," much higher than earthworms, says Patrick Zimmerman of the National Center for Atmospheric Research. They can break down 65 to 95 percent of the carbon in the wood they ingest. (Wood is 50 percent carbon.) And they can excrete phenomenal amounts of methane—a single mound might give off five liters a minute. As the deforestation has proceeded, termite numbers have boomed. There is now, some scientists estimate, a half ton of termites for every man, woman, and child on earth—that is, six or seven people's worth of termites for every actual person.

Researchers differ on the importance of termites as a methane source, but everyone agrees about the rice paddies. The oxygenless mud of marsh bottoms has always sheltered methane-producing bacteria. (Methane is sometimes known as swamp gas.) But rice paddies may be even more efficient—the rice plants act almost like straws, venting as much as 115 million tons of the gas a year. Rice paddies, of course, increase in number and size every year, so that those 2.4 children per Chinese woman will have enough to eat.

And then there are landfills: 30 percent of a typical landfill is "putrescible," Zimmerman says—it rots, creating methane. At the main New York City landfill on Staten Island, gas is pumped from under the trash straight to thousands of homes, but in most places it just seeps out.

What's more, scientists have recently begun to think that these sources alone can't account for all the methane. "If you look more carefully," the Harvard physicist Michael McElroy says, "you do not come away with an awfully comfortable feeling." For one thing, scientists have begun to be able to measure isotopic concentrations: there is a "light" methane from cattle and termites and rice paddies, but also a "heavy" methane from someplace else. And here—forget the poison-squirting termites—is where the story begins to get a little scary. An enormous amount of methane is locked up as hydrates in the tundra and in the mud of the continental shelves. These are, in essence, methane ices; the ocean muds alone may hold 10 trillion tons of methane. If the greenhouse effect is beginning to warm the oceans, if it is starting to thaw the permafrost, then some scientists say that eventually those ices could start to melt. Some estimates of the potential methane release run as high as .6 billion tons a year, an amount that could more than double the present atmospheric concentration. This would be a nasty example of a feedback loop, with the altered atmosphere causing further alterations: Warm the atmosphere and release methane; release methane and warm the atmosphere; and so on.

When all sources are combined, we've done an even more dramatic job of increasing methane than of increasing carbon dioxide. Samples of ice from Antarctic glaciers show that the concentration of methane in the atmosphere has fluctuated between 0.3 and 0.7 parts per million for the last 160,000 years, reaching its highest levels during earth's warmest period. In 1987 methane composed 1.7 parts per million of the atmosphere. That is, there is now two and a half times as much methane in the atmosphere as there was at any time through three glacial and interglacial periods. And concentrations are rising at a regular 1 percent a year.

Man is also pumping smaller quantities of many other greenhouse gases into the atmosphere. Nitrous oxide, chlorine compounds, and some others all trap warmth even more efficiently than carbon dioxide. Scientists now believe that methane and the rest of these gases, though their concentrations are small, will together account for 50 percent of the projected greenhouse warming—that is, taken together they are as much of a problem as carbon dioxide. And as all these compounds warm the atmosphere, it will be able to hold more water vapor, itself a potent greenhouse gas. The British Meteorological Office calculates that this extra water vapor will warm the earth two-thirds as much as the carbon dioxide alone.

So—WE HAVE INCREASED the amount of carbon dioxide in the air by about 25 percent in the last century, and will almost certainly double it in the next; we have more than doubled the level of methane; we have added a soup of other gases. *We have substantially altered the earth's atmosphere.*

This is not like local pollution, not like smog over Los Angeles. This is the earth's entire atmosphere. If you'd climbed some remote mountain in 1960 and sealed up a bottle of air at its peak, and did the same thing this year, the two samples would be substantially different. Their basic chemistry would have changed. Most discussions of the greenhouse gases rush immediately to their future consequences—is the sea going to rise?—without pausing to let the simple fact of what has already happened sink in. The air around us, even where it is clean, and smells like spring, and is filled with birds, is *different*, significantly changed.

That said, the question of what this new atmosphere means must arise. If it means nothing, we'd soon forget about it, since the air would be as colorless and odorless as before and as easy to breathe. And, indeed, the direct effects *are* unnoticeable. Anyone who lives indoors breathes carbon dioxide at a level several times the atmospheric concentration without ill effects; the federal government limits industrial workers to a chronic exposure of five thousand parts per million, or almost fifteen times the current atmospheric levels; a hundred years from now a child at recess will still breathe far less carbon dioxide than a child in a classroom.

This, however, is only mildly good news. The effects on us will be slightly less direct, but nevertheless drastic: changes in the atmosphere will change the weather, and *that* will change recess. The temperature, the rainfall, the speed of the wind will change. The chemistry of the upper atmosphere may seem an abstraction, a text written in a foreign language. But its translation into the weather of New York and Cincinnati and San Francisco will alter the lives of all of us.

The theories about the effects all begin with an estimate of expected warming. Arrhenius, you recall, said that doubling the preindustrial concentration of carbon dioxide would raise temperatures 9 degrees. The new wave of concern that began with Revelle and Suess's article and Keeling's Mauna Loa data has led to the development of vastly complex computer models of the entire globe. In those models the globe is divided into thousands of boxes, and each box is divided vertically into a large number of layers, usually ten or more, representing the various layers of the atmosphere and then of the land or ocean. The computer program, a sort of meteorological spreadsheet, first solves for each box the fundamental conservation laws of physics, and then goes on to calculate the transfer of mass, energy, and momentum from one box to the next—it "runs" the weather far into the future. You can change a variable— the amount of carbon dioxide in the air, for instance—and watch the result.

And the result, when increased carbon dioxide and other trace gases are taken as givens, does not differ all that much from what Arrhenius forecast. *The models that have been constructed agree that when, as has been predicted, the level of carbon dioxide or its equivalent in other greenhouse gases doubles from pre–Industrial Revolution concentrations, the global average temperature will increase, and that the increase will be 1.5 to 4.5 degrees Celsius, or 3 to 8 degrees Fahrenheit.* The results of all the global climatic models are consistent within a factor of two.

Perhaps the most famous of the computer programs is in the hands of James Hansen and his colleagues at NASA's Goddard Institute for Space Studies, in, of all places, Manhattan. NASA used an early version of the model around 1970 to study the accuracy of predictions from satellite weather observations; when the Goddard weather group moved to Washington, Hansen, who was staying on in New York, decided he'd try the model on longer-term problems—on climate as opposed to weather. Over the years, he and his colleagues have fine-tuned the program, and even though it remains a rough simulation of the mightily complex real world, they have improved it to the point where they are willing to forecast not just the effects of a doubling of carbon dioxide but the incremental effects along the way—that is, the forecast not just for 2050 but for 2000.

In Dallas, for instance, a doubled level of carbon dioxide, or the equivalent combination of carbon dioxide and other gases like methane, would increase the number of days a year with temperatures above 100 degrees from 19 to 78 each year, according to Hansen's calculations. On 68 days, as opposed to the current 4, the temperature wouldn't fall below 80 degrees at night. One hundred and sixty-two days a year—half the year, essentially—the temperature would top 90 degrees. New York City would have 48 days a year above the 90-degree mark, up from 15 at present. And so on. Such increases would quite clearly change the world as we know it. One of Hansen's colleagues observed to reporters, "It reaches one hundred twenty degrees in Phoenix now. Will people still live there if it's one hundred thirty degrees? One hundred forty?" (Heat waves like that are possible, even if the average global increase, figured over a year, is only a couple of degrees, for any average conceals huge swings.) But we need not wait decades for that doubling to occur. These changes, Hansen and his colleagues wrote in a paper published in the fall of 1988 in the *International Journal of Geophysics*, should begin to be obvious to the man in the street by the early 1990s at the latest—that is, the odds of a very hot summer will, thanks to the greenhouse effect, be better than even beginning now.

There are an infinite number of possible effects of such a temperature change. For example, the seas may well rise seven feet or more as polar ice melts and warmer water expands, while the interiors of the continents may dry up because of increased evaporation. Detailed studies have begun to emerge of what it will be like to live in this greenhouse world, and researchers have speculated on possible changes ranging from an increased spread of disease when insects spread north to the emergence of a warmer Canada as the globe's great power. Some of the figuring is quite insane—*Fortune* recently pointed out that if parts of the polar ice cap began to thaw, American and Soviet nuclear submarines would be deprived of cover. Not only that: "The effect would be more damaging to the USSR. Because American submarines are faster and can travel farther than their Soviet counterparts, they are less dependent on hiding places under the ice cap."

But a discussion of the effects is premature. First, we should figure out if this is indeed going to happen, if the theory is valid. In recent years there have been, of course, any number of doom-laden prophecies that haven't come true—oil is selling, as I write these words, at $18 per barrel, half its price just a few years ago.

The obvious check is to measure the temperature to see if it's going up. But this is easier said than done, for, in the first place, the warming doesn't show up immediately. Although, as Revelle and Suess found, the oceans don't absorb much excess carbon dioxide, they can hold a lot of heat; the effects so far may be stored up in the seas, ready to re-radiate out to the atmosphere, the way a rock holds the sun's heat through the night. Such a "thermal lag" could be as little as ten years, as much as a hundred.

And when you go to check the thermometers it won't do to measure only a few places for only a few years because climate is "noisy"—full of random fluctuations and variability. To find what climatologists call the "warming signal" through this static of naturally cold and hot years requires a huge effort. Two such studies have been done, one at the University of East Anglia, the other by Hansen and his NASA colleagues. Each reached back almost a century, when scientists first began systematic weather observations. And, to find truly global averages, they included readings from thousands of land-based and shipboard monitoring stations. The two studies reached about the same conclusion: that the earth's temperature had increased about 1 degree Fahrenheit in the past hundred years, a number consistent with, though somewhat smaller than, the predictions of the greenhouse models. And both sets of readings show that the four warmest years on record occurred in the 1980s—that the rise is accelerating at the same time that more gases enter the air, just as the models forecast. Indeed, the British model now lists the six warmest years on record as, in order, 1988, 1987, 1983, 1981, 1980, and 1986.

THE YEARS 1981 and 1983 were very hot, and some parts of the United States suffered severe drought. But no one except the affected farmers worried very much. It was weather. Even the scientists most committed to the greenhouse theories made no claims; "it must be said," wrote Revelle in 1982, "that so far the warming trend has not risen above the 'noise level.' . . . Confidence in the carbon dioxide hypothesis will be much firmer if a warming trend exceeding the noise level becomes evident."

In 1988, though, the American drought caught everyone's attention. It hit the heart of the grain belt, where most of the nation's and much of the world's food is grown. It followed a dry fall and winter, so its effects were quickly evident; the Mississippi River, for instance, sank to its lowest level since the navy began taking measurements in 1872. And just about the time that the pictures on the television began to grab everyone's attention it got very, very hot in the urban East, where those in the government and the media establishment, among others, have their homes. It so happened that in late June, right as the anxiety was rising in a great crescendo— newscasters telling us that the next two weeks were crucial for corn fertilization, meteorologists issuing forlorn sixty-day forecasts—the Senate Committee on Energy and Natural Resources held a hearing on the greenhouse effect. It was actually the second part of the hearing. Part one had been held the previous November, when, in the words of Louisiana senator J. Bennett Johnston, the senators listened with "concern" as scientists said that one expected result of the greenhouse effect would be a drying of the Midwest. But now, said Senator Johnston, "as we experience 101-degree temperatures in Washington, D.C., and the [lack of] soil moisture across the midwest is ruining the soybean crops, the corn crops, the cotton crops," "concern" is giving way to "alarm."

As at most congressional hearings, some of the senators on the panel made opening remarks before the witnesses spoke. Several senators said they had already read the report of Dr. Hansen, the day's chief witness, and they predicted that it would startle listeners. Hansen's report, Dale Bumpers of Arkansas said, should be "cause for headlines in every newspaper in America tomorrow morning."

As it turned out, Senator Bumpers was not exaggerating. Hansen said he was ready to state, after exhaustive review of the records, that the warming signal was now apparent above the noise of normal weather. That there was only a 1 percent chance that the temperature increases seen in the last few years were accidental. That the theories and predictions had come true—that we now lived in the greenhouse world.

It was a claim no other established scientist had ever made—certainly not one on a government payroll. And though Hansen delivered his findings in the flat, dry tones of a good researcher, the reaction was much as the senators had expected: the next day's *New York Times*, for instance, ran a story at the top of the front page under the headline "Global Warming Has Begun, Expert Tells Senate." The message was finally getting across, nearly a century after Arrhenius and three decades past Revelle and Suess. But the heat of the day may have been a mixed blessing—though it focused everyone's attention on the issue, it led most people to think that what Hansen had said was that the heat and drought of 1988 were greenhouse related. Strictly speaking, that is not what he had testified to. "It is not possible to blame a specific drought on the greenhouse effect," he said. (Indeed many experts think that most of the drought and heat of 1988 was the result of tropical ocean currents and related natural phenomena.) However, said Hansen, there is evidence that the greenhouse effect "increases the likelihood of such events."

In other words, what we *can* blame the carbon dioxide and the methane for is a longer-range pattern. Even if the summer of 1988 had been cool and damp, even if there had been mushrooms growing in the wheat fields of Kansas, Hansen would have said the same thing. What had convinced him was not the anguished farmers of the Midwest or the ecstatic air-conditioner salesmen of the eastern cities, but the numbers his computer kept spitting at him. And if the next Fourth of July should see blizzards burying the Plains or even just the normal heat of an average summer, it might calm down those who still believe that the world is too big and too old to change, but it wouldn't shake Hansen's confidence in the implications of his hundred years' worth of thermometer readings.

"There are two logical time scales to consider," he explained some months after giving his testimony. "One is the thirty years for which we have some measurements of carbon dioxide and other gases. The natural variability in temperature for the years between 1950 and 1980 is about .13 degrees Celsius. And our readings show that the global mean temperature has risen about .4 degrees in that period. The other logical choice would be to look at the larger record, the observations back to the 1800s. Over that period there's been about a .6 degree Celsius rise. Now, over a longer period there's also more natural variability—sources like sunspots, deep ocean circulation, and so forth." The standard deviation, the randomness of temperature, over the longer period is plus or minus .2 degrees Celsius. In both cases, Hansen's observed rise was almost exactly three times the standard deviation. "There's no magic point where you pick out the signal," he said. "There's no point at which it switches over. But when it gets to three sigma—when it gets to three standard deviations—you're getting to a level where it's unlikely to be an accidental warming."

As the hearings closed for the day—after several other authorities supported his findings, forecast a wide range of effects (none pleasant), and called for strong action to reduce fossil fuel emissions—reporters gathered around the table asking questions. In response to one query, Hansen said, "It's time to stop waffling so much. It's time to say the earth is getting warmer."

WHETHER OR NOT the warming has officially begun is probably a more important point for the politicians than for the scientists. Only a few months before Hansen's testimony, the columnist George Will had spanked the then presidential candidate Senator Albert Gore of Tennessee for his long-held interest in the greenhouse effect and other issues "that are, in the eyes of the electorate, not even peripheral." Will and, presumably, his readership were still back in about 1975, when a National Academy of Sciences report, on *Understanding Climatic Change*, devoted only two paragraphs to carbon dioxide. For at least the last eight years, though, a consensus has been growing in the scientific community that while a warming trend might not yet have appeared, it was inevitable: the National Research Council, the Environmental Protection Agency, the World Meteorological Organization, the United Nations Environmental Programme, and many other scientific groups issued voluminous reports outlining the "projected," "predicted," "expected," "forecast" rise. The warming might have started or it might start a few years hence—if the theory was sound, it didn't make much difference. The language of a 1983 National Academy of Sciences report is typical of this hedging: "The available data on trends in globally or hemispherically averaged temperatures over the last century, together with estimates of carbon dioxide changes over the period, do not preclude the possibility that some climatic changes due to increasing atmospheric projections might already be underway." But "do not preclude," "possibility"—these are words that land a subject on *Nova*, not the *CBS Evening News*, and so 1988's summer heat, even if it were a freak unrelated to the composition of the atmosphere, was probably a necessary preliminary to any serious public discussion. It's the difference between knowing that your two packs a day could very well give you cancer and hearing the doctor clear his throat and say, "I've got something to tell you."

Many scientists, even among those committed to the greenhouse theory, believe that the warming signal is not yet evident. Hansen, though well respected, was out on a limb, if a fairly stout one, and some have criticized not only his use of statistics but his willingness to speak with few caveats. Stephen Schneider, of the National Center for Atmospheric Research in Boulder, Colorado, and a longtime proponent of the greenhouse warming theory, offers a gambler's analogy: the warm years of the 1980s, he said, are not "proof" of a warming, any more than the dealer's drawing four aces is "proof" that he's dealing from the bottom of the deck. "Different tastes cause people to accept the reality of a hypothesized climatic change at a low signal-to-noise ratio, whereas others might not believe in the reality of the change until it has persisted for a very long time," Schneider told the Senate six weeks after Hansen's testimony.

"Quite simply, accepting any particular signal-to-noise ratio as 'proof' of global warming reflects the personal judgment of the investigator." A scientific panel concluded in early May 1989 that natural variations in temperature made it impossible to say "with any degree of confidence" that a warming was officially under way.

Some recent studies tend to agree with Hansen's conclusion that the warming has already begun. Rainfall may have increased above 30 degrees north latitude and decreased beneath it, for instance, and there has been a "remarkable" increase in the amount of water vapor in the air over the Indo-Pacific, both results anticipated in the greenhouse models. And some investigators have found a "variable but widespread" warming of the Alaskan permafrost, which changes temperature much more slowly than the air and thus may provide a better record. On the other hand, some scientists have looked for the warming signal and found few indications of it so far. Kenneth E. F. Watt, a professor of environmental studies at the University of California at Davis, dismisses most of the Hansen and East Anglia temperature studies, saying, among other things, that they failed to correct enough for the "urban heat island effect," a phenomenon well known to meteorologists in which, as "cities grow up around thermometers," concrete and exhaust skew readings. (This heat island effect even has its converse—in Palm Springs, California, researchers reported that they had discovered a "cold island effect." Temperatures had dropped 2 to 3 degrees Fahrenheit below those of the surrounding desert, apparently because of a surge in golf-course construction.) Even shipboard measurements suffer from this pollution, and so the scientists try to correct for phenomena like the heating of water in engine intake tubes.

There's also no guarantee that factors much larger than the growth of cities aren't skewing the results—sunspots are a prime contender, as are the strong El Niño currents of recent years. Weather is a strong force. Most climatologists agree that the drought of 1988, for instance, was the result of regularly fluctuating tropical ocean temperatures, which steered the North American jet stream, with its cargo of rainstorms, north of the Great Plains. In fact, in January 1989 Tim Barnett, a climate researcher at the Scripps Institution of Oceanography in La Jolla, California, forecast much cooler temperatures for the first part of the year, the result of a one-year La Niña, a tropical "cold event" that is the opposite of the better-known El Niño. In some parts of the ocean off equatorial South America the water temperature plunged nearly 7 degrees Fahrenheit last summer; Hansen saw the dip in his computer data, and agrees that it may make this year's readings go up more slowly, or perhaps even go down. "But such things are bumps," he says. The greenhouse effect is superimposed on top of them, like makeup on a face.

At any rate, there are very few objections to the theory as a whole; everyone in the scientific community agrees that the atmospheric concentration of carbon dioxide is on the rise, and almost everyone believes that it cannot help having some effect. To declare, as some editorialists have done, that the warming has not yet appeared and therefore the theory is wrong is like arguing that a woman hasn't yet given birth and therefore isn't pregnant.

A year after Hansen's original testimony, in May of 1989, he returned to Capitol Hill to declare that his studies showed definite danger of future drought. The White House tried to alter his testimony, arguing that, in the words of presidential press secretary Marlin Fitzwater, "There are many points of view on the global warming issue." But he didn't point to any studies undercutting Hansen's work, and the next day another government scientist, Schneider of the National Center for Atmospheric Research, assured the assembled congressmen that "there is virtually no scientific controversy" that more carbon dioxide means higher temperatures. "This is not," he said, "a speculative theory."

THE ACCEPTED SCIENTIFIC WISDOM, then, is that the increase in carbon dioxide and other trace gases will soon heat the world if it hasn't already done so. The consensus begins to break down, though, on the question of what happens after that. A large-scale change in the climate would undoubtedly set off a series of other changes, and some of these, in turn, would make the problem worse, while others might lessen it. Skeptics incline toward the latter view—to think that there is a possibility that the warming will trigger some natural compensatory brake. S. Fred Singer, a professor emeritus of environmental sciences at the University of Virginia, who is now chief scientist for the federal Department of Transportation, has also assumed a part-time role as greenhouse curmudgeon, expressing his doubts on various op-ed pages. He grants that the earth's temperature should increase "provided all other factors remain the same." But, he says, they won't. "For example, as oceans warm and more water vapor enters the atmosphere, the greenhouse effect will increase somewhat, but so should cloudiness—which can keep out incoming solar radiation and thereby reduce the warming." There are other possibilities. If changing climatic conditions caused the oceans to circulate water from the bottom to the top more quickly than the present five-hundred-year cycle, "older" water that could absorb a certain amount more carbon dioxide might reach the surface. Or higher levels of carbon dioxide might stimulate plant growth, thus pulling more carbon dioxide from the air. "The feedbacks are enormously complicated," Michael MacCracken, of California's Lawrence Livermore National Laboratory, told reporters. "It's like a Rube Goldberg machine in the sense of the number of things that interact in order to tip the world into fire and ice."

The computer models have tried to incorporate such factors. In some cases, Hansen admits, we simply don't have enough knowledge to do more than make educated guesses—the behavior of the oceans *is* something of a wild card, and so are the clouds (the difficulty of estimating cloud feedbacks is a major reason that most warming predictions are expressed as a range of temperatures and not as a single, firm number). But almost every doubt is double edged. It's true that some types of clouds—bright, low-level stratocumulus clouds, say—reflect a lot of solar radiation and might tend to cool the earth. Monsoon clouds, on the other hand, are long and thin, and let in the sun's heat while preventing its escape. Hansen's work shows that clouds will most likely increase the greenhouse warming overall.

A variety of other feedback effects have also been identified and tallied up. For instance, every surface has its "albedo," the degree to which it reflects the sun's rays. A polar ice cap (or a white shirt) has a high albedo—a large proportion of the sun's rays are immediately reflected back out to space. If the ice is replaced by dark blue ocean, more heat will be absorbed. Tropical rain forests absorb a lot of heat now; if they turn into deserts they may reflect more. The feedbacks are distinct from other phenomena that have always affected and will always affect temperature—volcanoes, for instance, which throw up so much dust that it acts as a veil, or El Niños, or increased radiance from solar flares. The various feedbacks are, rather, products of the warming signal, and they can either amplify or mute it.

In any event, the warming estimates provided by the greenhouse models are *not* worst-case scenarios. They are the middle ground. It is "equally likely," Schneider told the Senate, that the warming forecasts are too low as that they're too high.

SOME OF THE POTENTIAL FEEDBACKS are so vast that they might someday make us almost forget what originally caused the greenhouse warming. We have already looked at one: the potential release of the methane trapped in the tundra and the mud of the sea that would add enormously to the warming blanket around the earth.

But methane is a little hard to imagine. It's easier—and more troubling—for me to think about the forest that surrounds my house in New York State's Adirondack Mountains.

Twenty thousand years ago, my land was covered by glaciers which had spread slowly down from Canada, and which eventually retreated in the same direction. As the ice disappeared, in the words of a local writer, "the fierce ruthlessness of nature gave way to a benevolent mood. Rains came over the years to chasten the harshness of the landscape. The startling gaping holes in the earth were filled with crystal-clear water. Soft green foliage came to clothe the naked rock-hewn slopes." This was a slow (albeit poetic) process, even now incomplete—some plant and animal species are still migrating up here. The great forests rose on the glacial till and soon created more soil for greater forests, and so on, a process first interrupted a couple of hundred years ago, when men cut down most of the woods. But the interruption was only temporary—around the turn of the century, New York State, in an early outburst of environmental consciousness, began buying huge tracts of land and declaring them "forever wild"—off limits to loggers and condo developers alike. As a result, it is one of those happy exceptions: a reforested, replenished zone, a second-chance wilderness.

But the trees that live here don't do so because of the laws—they do so because of the climate. They have slowly marched north as the climate slowly warmed since the end of the Ice Age, and if it continued slowly warming they would slowly keep marching; the convoy of pines might march right out of here, and the mass of hardwoods found in lower Appalachian latitudes might eventually march in to replace them. But before we get too used to this marching metaphor it is worth recalling that trees are rooted to the ground—they die looking out at the sights they were born to. And, as forests are composed of trees, they can move only through the slow growth of new trees along their edges. In fact, researchers estimate that a forest naturally moves at most a half mile in a year. Which is fine, if that's how slowly the climate is changing.

The computer models, however, project an increase in global average temperature as high as a degree Fahrenheit per decade. An increase of 1 degree in average temperature moves the climatic zones thirty-five to fifty miles north—that's why, when you drive from Atlanta to New York the vegetation that lines the highways changes. So, if the temperature was increasing a degree per decade, the forest surrounding my home here would be due at the Canadian border sometime around 2020, which is just about the time that we'd be expecting the trees from a hundred miles south to start arriving. They won't—half a mile a year, remember, is as fast as forests move. The trees outside my window will still be there; it's just that they'll be dead or dying.

Eventually, perhaps within a few decades, forests—or, at least, scrub—better adapted to the new conditions would replace the forests that had expired. But in the meantime those dead forests could release truly staggering amounts of carbon into the atmosphere. Trees are largely carbon—the burning of the tropical rain forests releases up to 3 billion tons a year into the atmosphere, compared with about 5.6 billion tons from the burning of fossil fuels. Last year's Yellowstone fire alone released an estimated 2.8 percent as much carbon as all U.S. emissions from fossil fuels in a year—that is, in a few weeks, on only about a million and a half acres, the fires released as much carbon as ten days' worth of driving, home heating, factory production, motorboating, and so on. All told, the forests, plants, and soil (which gives up its carbon much more rapidly as trees die) contain something more than 2 trillion tons of carbon, probably more than a third of it in the middle and high latitudes. "We're working with maybe a trillion tons that could be mobilized," says George Woodwell, an ecologist and the director of the Woods Hole Research Center. By contrast, the atmosphere now contains only about 750 billion tons. So even a fairly small change in the forests could substantially increase the amount of carbon in the atmosphere, exacerbating the warming. There are signs—frightening signs—that some of these feedback loops are starting to kick in, that the warm years of the 1980s may be triggering an endless cycle. In May 1989 Woodwell told Congress that the annual 1.5 parts per million in atmospheric carbon dioxide seemed to have suddenly surged upward in the last eighteen months to 2.5 parts per million. "I'm suggesting that the warming of the earth is increasing the decay of organic matter," he said, adding that such an event has not been worked into the computer climate models and hence their estimates of future warming may be too low.

But forget the carbon for a moment, forget the feedback loops. The trees will die. Consider nothing more than that—just that the trees will die. When I walk outdoors in the morning, instead of the slopes of trees, instead of the craggy white pines on the ridge toward Buck Hill, there may be yellowing and browning leaves and needles, thinning crowns, dead branches, and rotting stumps. Or maybe, after what the World Resources Institute calls a "transition period," a "shrubby woodland that is adapted to a wider variety of environmental conditions" will appear. It may be personal prejudice, nothing more, but I prefer trees to shrubs. You can keep your sumac bush—give me yellow birch, tamarack, blue spruce, the swamp maple first to change its color in the fall, rock maple, hemlock. This vast decline, this forest "dieback," is not some distant proposition. A report described to a congressional committee last summer found that "reproductive failure and forest dieback is estimated to begin between 2000 and 2050." A University of Virginia study predicted what Michael Oppenheimer of the Environmental Defense Fund called "biomass crashes" in the pine forests of the Southeast over the next forty years if the warming continues. "Things like birch trees and many evergreens [in the Northeast] may have a hard time surviving, even in the next ten to twenty years," Hansen told reporters.

WHEN TREES DIE, it is always hard, unfortunately, to say just why. "It's never going to be obvious that the climate change is doing it," Woodwell says. "Pine trees are often attacked by a boring insect, the ips. The insects come from miles around to a weakened tree. So when it dies, people say it was an ips infestation. Sugar maples are going out all over—acid rain, and the accumulation of heavy metals like aluminum in the soils, and then the pear thrip, which is another insect that goes after weak trees. In every case it looks like some special cause—a fungus or a pest." Alf Johnnels, of the Swedish Museum of Natural History, compared the situation to a famine: "There are relatively few people who die directly from starvation; they die from dysentery or various infectious diseases."

In one sense it makes no difference. The tree is dead one way or another, and the carbon released. But in another way it is tragic, for it masks a vital piece of knowledge—the transition from "traditional" pollutants to these new horrors whose causes and effects are everywhere. When Eleanor of Aquitaine, wife of King Henry II, moved out of Tutbury Castle in Nottingham because of the smoke from wood stoves; when London, as early as the thirteenth century, barred coal combustion because of the smog; when Lake Erie nearly died—all these were traditional pollutants, local in their effect, obvious in their action, their sources relatively easy to identify and, often, to deal with. Love Canal; the lethal smog in Donora, Pennsylvania; the acid streams in the coal country of West Virginia—all traditional pollution.

But in the late 1960s and early 1970s, people in Scandinavia and the northeastern United States began to notice damage to forests in areas a long way from any obvious source of pollution. Eventually, they began to measure the pH of rainfall, and of the lakes where the rain collected. What they found was startling: the rainfall was turning acid. Its pH, normally around 5.6, often fell below 5.0. Measurements of clouds around mountaintops showed that in their acidity they resembled vinegar or lemon juice, not water vapor.

Acid rain was not a new concept or even a new phrase; Robert Angus Smith, the inspector general of the Alkali Inspectorate for the United Kingdom, coined the term in the late nineteenth century. His data on the chemistry of rainfall around Europe correlated nicely with his maps of heavy coal-burning regions and strong wind currents. He even speculated that the acid rainfall might damage trees. But, like the calculations of Arrhenius, the notion was forgotten immediately, and not remembered until quite recently. (Until 1986, Britain itself relied on ten thousand schoolchildren with lemonade bottles to collect its rainwater for analysis.)

And even when many researchers in the 1970s and 1980s did begin to point to coal burning as the culprit, they had a hard time making headway with their arguments, for acid rain, besides being colorless, tasteless, and odorless, is not a traditional pollutant. It comes from a distance to do its damage. Or, really, it's halfway between a traditional pollutant and the new sources of environmental destruction, like the global warming. In some ways it's the same old coal smoke that has always darkened urban areas. But to get the nasty stuff out of sight (and, it was hoped, mind) the electric utilities, whose generating stations cause most of the problem, built ever-taller smokestacks—429 stacks taller than two hundred feet (many of them taller than seven hundred feet) were built in the midwestern and southeastern United States in the 1970s. Since the emissions spew out high above the ground, winds carry them great distances—hundreds, even thousands, of miles. Under the right conditions, sulfur dioxide and nitrogen oxides in the emissions are transmuted into nitric and sulfuric acid that eventually drift to the ground or fall in the rain. And there they weaken the trees and acidify the lakes to the point of sterility.

There is no question that the damage is increasing. Between 1964 and 1979 half the mid- to high-elevation red spruce trees in Vermont died; in Sweden all bodies of fresh water are now acidic, roughly fifteen thousand of them too sour to support aquatic life; rainfall in southern China has grown more acidic than the badly damaged parts of the Atlantic seaboard; even in the American West the pH of rainfall has plummeted to the point where two-thirds of the region's lakes now have "limited acid-neutralizing capacity." Central Europe, small and highly industrialized, has perhaps been hardest hit. When the Worldwatch Institute was working on its first State of the World Report in 1983, recalled director Lester Brown, and staff member Christopher Flavin, it "debated whether to report that a West German forest survey had found some eight percent of that nation's forests showing signs of damage, possibly from air pollution and acid rain. That discovery, though disturbing, seemed little cause for international alarm." But by 1988—that is, five years later—"over one-half of West Germany's forests are damaged, and the link to air pollution is all but conclusive."

Still, for a decade or more, nothing was done save studies. And partly this was because, for the first time, the people doing the polluting were at some remove from the pollution. In such a situation the usual environmental ideas don't work, because the problem is outside our normal way of thinking. For some years one of the chief (and admirable) slogans of environmentalists has been "Think globally, act locally." It is true that one can work most effectively close to home instead of futilely addressing all the world's problems. But as the reality changes, so must the perception. Our local problem here in the Adirondacks—acid rain—has its cause in Ohio and Kentucky. And now, as the climate warms, our local problem—the death of trees—starts to have its causes everywhere. *Everywhere.* A factory in Japan is as deadly as a burning rain forest in Brazil, a Communist coal mine in Romania, a capitalist utility in West Virginia. Or as the blue 1981 Honda parked in the driveway twenty feet from where I sit, or as the wood stove warming my back.

THE BEST EXAMPLE of the global nature of the new pollution is probably the depletion of the ozone layer. Ozone, or O_3, is a molecule in which three oxygen atoms are bound together. It is formed in the stratosphere when intense ultraviolet solar radiation splits ordinary oxygen molecules, O_2, into their two constituent atoms. When that happens, most of the oxygen atoms simply recombine as O_2, but some join as triplets and others adhere to O_2 molecules, in both cases forming ozone. Ozone in turn absorbs ultraviolet radiation. That radiation tears it apart, forming O_2 and O, and the dance continues, with all the elements in balance in the atmosphere, and much of the incoming ultraviolet absorbed—fortunately, since too much ultraviolet can damage plant and animal cells, causing, among humans, skin cancer and eye damage, and killing many smaller and more sensitive organisms.

This dance had gone on uninterrupted since the Archean era, a span of time measured in billions of years. Then, in 1928, a group of chemists at General Motors invented a nontoxic gas, a combination of carbon, chlorine, and fluorine atoms, which they labeled a chlorofluorocarbon, or CFC. (The group was led by Thomas Midgley, who also advanced the human race by formulating tetraethyl lead as a gasoline additive, and who may now hold the record for most banned substances produced by a single man.) The chlorofluorocarbons, though perhaps the ultimate proof that what is good for General Motors is not good for America, seemed at first to have a number of desirable features: they could be used as coolants in refrigerators, and also as propellant gases in spray cans. Since they were inert, they didn't affect the contents of what they propelled—when you pushed the button on the green can it sprayed green paint. The number of CFC compounds quickly grew into the dozens, of which CFC 11 and CFC 12 (the numbering system, devised by the DuPont Company, refers to the number of fluorine and chlorine atoms) were the most commercially important. The chlorofluorocarbons are now used for a wide variety of jobs. Besides refrigerating 75 percent of the food consumed in the United States, and propelling much of the world's aerosol spray, they serve as foaming agents for plastics and as cleaning agents for computer circuit boards, they fumigate granaries and cargo holds, and they insulate pipelines and trucks. And they make egg cartons, and those foam coffee cups and fast-food packages.

Chlorofluorocarbons have been effectively marketed even to individual consumers—for instance, some automobile dealers send out annual notices urging that their customers come have their air conditioners flushed and the CFC coolant replaced, even though this is generally unnecessary. Between 1958 and 1983 the average production of CFC 11 and CFC 12 grew 13 percent a year, and could continue to grow more or less indefinitely, since large reserves of fluorspar, the source of the key ingredient, have been located.

However, besides being inert, nontoxic, and widely useful, chlorofluorocarbons have a pair of other unusual properties. One is that, unlike many chemicals in the atmosphere that decay in hours, days, weeks, or months, the CFCs are so chemically unreactive that they often can stay intact for a century or more. (CFC 11 lasts seventy-five years on the average, and CFC 12 a hundred and ten.) This gives them plenty of time to rise slowly through the atmosphere until they reach the stratospheric altitudes, a process that may take five years. And when they get there, they react chemically with the ozone molecules, destroying them. For instance, a single atom of chlorine in the CFCs may react with ozone—O_3—to create a molecule of O_2 and a molecule of chlorine monoxide. Then, in a second reaction, the chlorine monoxide reacts with a single oxygen molecule (O) to form O_2 and the single atom of chlorine is freed again, to seek out and destroy more ozone. A single molecule of chlorine can destroy thousands of ozone molecules.

And just as methane joins carbon dioxide to warm the atmosphere, several other compounds, including methyl chloroform and carbon tetrachloride, assist the CFCs in ozone destruction. Methyl chloroform and carbon tetrachloride are solvents. Another family of man-made compounds, the halons, are popular as home fire extinguishers because they don't cause water damage. But they contain bromines, which are a hundred times more efficient than the chlorine compounds at ozone destruction. Therefore, though there are many fewer home fire extinguishers than air conditioners, the halons may cause a quarter of the ozone loss.

SCIENTISTS FIRST BEGAN to think seriously about the chlorofluorocarbons (which, like carbon dioxide, also trap heat) in the early 1970s. James Lovelock, the independent British scientist best known for formulating the Gaia hypothesis, which holds that the earth is a single living organism, was the first to measure the chemicals in the air. He showed that they were both widespread and persistent in the earth's atmosphere, but concluded, in what he later described as "one of my greatest blunders," that "the presence of these compounds constitutes no conceivable hazard." A year or two later, Sherwood F. Rowland of the University of California at Irvine, and Mario Molina, now at the Jet Propulsion Laboratory in Pasadena, first demonstrated the ozone-destroying capability of the chlorine atoms and suggested the magnitude of the problem. Rowland has recalled, "I just came home one night and told my wife, 'The work is going very well, but it looks like the end of the world.' " Their findings—especially the vision of a nation underarm-deodorizing its way to total destruction, expiring not with a bang but with a floral hiss—led to an American decision to ban chlorofluorocarbons as an aerosol propellant. However, most of the rest of the world continued to spray, and the compounds continued to be used for other purposes; their use continued at an almost uninterrupted double-digit rate of annual growth.

The problem, as with carbon dioxide and the warming, is that there was more theory than observation. Not that anyone had much quarrel with the theory, but political action had to wait for some major scare. The Vienna Convention of 1985, for instance, brought together all sorts of countries, which agreed on the "general obligation" to control CFCs but took no actual action. The United States, Canada, and several European countries wanted an aerosol ban (since they already had one); most of the Europeans, though, wanted a reduction in aerosol uses and some hazy cap on future production. Pending a decision on a specific protocol, the meeting was content to urge countries to control emissions "to the maximum extent practicable." Then, two months after that vague manifesto, the British Antarctic Survey at Halley Bay, which had been monitoring the Antarctic stratosphere since 1957, reported that a huge hole had suddenly developed in the ozone high above the South Pole. Actually, it was not so sudden: American Nimbus monitoring satellites had been recording the hole for at least five years, but the computers had been instructed to ignore sharp changes like the one observed in the ozone. (Men and women in the street have no monopoly on complacency. Scientists who program computers are like the rest of us—they expect that if nature changes at all it will do so slowly and steadily. Anomalous results, they assume, mean broken instruments and not a broken world.) "All along," Rowland said, "critics complained that ozone depletion was not based on real atmospheric measurements—until, that is, the ozone hole appeared. Now we're not talking about ozone losses in 2050. We're talking about losses last year."

Rowland and Molina's models had not predicted the Antarctic ozone hole that the British found, and for a while some scientists believed that the window (perhaps too homey a phrase for something the size of the continental United States) was a natural phenomenon of the pole. Since it appeared at the same time each year—September and October—they postulated some climatic cause. But in 1987 an international team of researchers established once and for all that man-made chemicals were what caused the ozone loss. It appears that global winds tend to move air from the equator to the poles, carrying the CFCs with them. During the Antarctic winters, according to Harvard's McElroy, the difference in temperatures between the middle latitudes and the poles forms a strong pressure gradient that starts the air moving. This spinning air forms large-scale vortices of cyclonelike winds, with temperatures inside dropping as low as minus 130 degrees Fahrenheit. Clouds of microscopic ice crystals form in these vortices, and chemicals are produced on their surfaces that are responsible for the very rapid destruction of ozone. Inside the vortices as much as 50 percent of the ozone may disappear. And then, as the vortex breaks up after a month and a half, its low-ozone air mixes with the surrounding atmosphere, lowering the earth's overall ozone level. It's like watering down beer. According to McElroy, the world has lost between 1 and 3 percent of its ozone. In 1987 scientists noticed the first signs that a similar hole develops in the height of the Arctic winter—that is especially because the areas adjacent to the North Pole are much more densely populated than those around the South. Already, monitoring stations in spots as far apart as North Dakota and Switzerland have recorded wintertime drops in the ozone layer of up to 9 percent. And a study conducted by a NASA Ozone Trends panel early in 1988 concluded that stratospheric ozone levels in the Northern Hemisphere had declined as much as 3 percent in the last twenty years—much more than the models predicted. By 1987, global ozone depletion was at the level forecast for the 2020s.

The ozone hole was enough of a shock that many politicians urged action. (Not all—the Reagan administration's interior secretary Donald Hodel urged that Americans who were worried about skin cancer and retina damage simply don baseball caps and sunglasses.) In a follow-up to the Vienna Convention, diplomats agreed in a document known as the Montreal protocol to a 50 percent reduction in chlorofluorocarbon production to be phased in by century's end. That was pretty radical action. The accord, noted the Worldwatch Institute in its generally gloomy State of the World 1988 survey, represents "an important psychological victory. . . . It indicates that the international community is capable of cooperating when faced with a common threat." Unfortunately, that unprecedented level of cooperation would still allow the level of ozone-destroying chlorine in the atmosphere to increase dramatically.

A report released in 1988 by the Environmental Policy Institute concluded that only a rapid and total phaseout of all ozone-destroying chemicals could begin to stabilize ozone levels in the next few decades. Chemical companies, needless to say, have not been overjoyed at such a prospect. "The rapid, complete shutdown of CFCs that some people are calling for would have horrendous consequences," said a spokesman for the Alliance for a Responsible CFC Policy, an industry arm, adding, in an odd choice of metaphor, "The cure would kill the patient." Still, the leading CFC producers finally announced they're searching for substitutes so they can leave the business. And the EPA seems convinced. Even before the Montreal accord took effect, the agency concluded that its provisions would allow chlorine levels to triple, and in September 1988 EPA administrator Lee Thomas called for a quick phaseout of CFC production and a freeze on the other ozone-destroying chemicals. British prime minister Margaret Thatcher, though she took many years to see the danger, has said that the halfway cuts are not enough; at a major ozone conference in London in the spring of 1989 she led the way in urging a total ban.

Anything less will clearly be insufficient. Under the Montreal accord, "we're on an upward ramp that will level off at about ten percent depletion," said Michael Oppenheimer of the Environmental Defense Fund. "We're headed rapidly into the realm of dangerous UV radiation." No exact map of that realm exists. Not even the scariest models predicted anything like the Antarctic hole. The Environmental Policy Institute lists as a worst-case scenario the possibility that as much as 25 percent of the atmosphere's ozone could be depleted by the middle of the next century unless emissions are cut dramatically. (A nuclear war, by contrast, would destroy 30 to 70 percent of the ozone layer.) If ozone levels declined 20 percent, two hours in the sun would blister exposed skin.

For THE MOMENT, however, forget about effects. The physical consequences of increasing the level of carbon dioxide and lowering the amount of ozone in the atmosphere will in some cases be staggering, but they are no more staggering than the simple fact of what we have done. Look at them one way and the changes are small enough. Carbon dioxide will increase, if it doubles in concentration, from .035 percent of the atmosphere to .06 or .07 percent of the atmosphere. If all the ozone currently above a particular spot on the globe were compressed to atmospheric pressure, it would be a tenth of an inch thick; in the nastiest of futures it might shrink to perhaps a twelfth of an inch. But the level has already shrunk, if only by a percent or two. It is different, markedly different, different everywhere on earth.

And the changes—many of them, at least—are irrevocable. They are not possibilities. They cannot be wished away and they cannot be legislated away. To prevent them, we would have had to clean up our collective act many decades ago. Though scientists disagree about whether or not the warming has begun, they do not argue that carbon dioxide hasn't increased, or that the increase won't have an effect. The "thermal equilibrium"—the heat storage—of the oceans may be saving us at the moment. But if so it is only a sort of chemical budget deficit. Sooner or later our loans will be called in. The latest estimates predict that man's release *to date* of carbon dioxide and other gases will warm the atmosphere as little as 1 degree Fahrenheit or as much as 2.8. And we continue, of course, to burn oil and cut trees and grow rice.

We have done this ourselves, by driving our cars, building our factories, cutting down our forests, turning on our air conditioners. The exact physical effects of our alterations—even whether or not they will be for the worse—are for the moment beside the point. They will be dealt with in the second half of this book, which is about the future. For now, simply recognize the magnitude of what we have done. In the years since the Civil War, and mostly in the years since World War II, we have changed the atmosphere— changed it enough so that the climate will change dramatically. Most of the major events of human history have gradually lost their meaning: wars that seemed at the time all important are now a series of dates that schoolchildren don't even try to remember; great feats of engineering now crumble in the desert. Man's efforts, even at their mightiest, were tiny compared with the size of the planet— the Roman Empire meant nothing to the Arctic or the Amazon. But now, the way of life of one part of the world in one half century is altering every inch and every hour of the globe.

The End of Nature

ALMOST EVERY DAY, I hike up the hill out my back door. Within a hundred yards the woods swallows me up, and there is nothing to remind me of human society—no trash, no stumps, no fence, not even a real path. Looking out from the high places, you can't see road or house; it is a world apart from man. But once in a while someone will be cutting wood farther down the valley, and the snarl of a chain saw will fill the woods. It is harder on those days to get caught up in the timeless meaning of the forest, for man is nearby. The sound of the chain saw doesn't blot out all the noises of the forest or drive the animals away, but it does drive away the feeling that you are in another, separate, timeless, wild sphere.

Now that we have changed the most basic forces around us, the noise of that chain saw will always be in the woods. We have changed the atmosphere, and that will change the weather. The temperature and rainfall are no longer to be entirely the work of some separate, uncivilizable force, but instead in part a product of our habits, our economies, our ways of life. Even in the most remote wilderness, where the strictest laws forbid the felling of a single tree, the sound of that saw will be clear, and a walk in the woods will be changed—tainted—by its whine. The world outdoors will mean much the same thing as the world indoors, the hill the same thing as the house.

An idea, a relationship, can go extinct, just like an animal or a plant. The idea in this case is "nature," the separate and wild province, the world apart from man to which he adapted, under whose rules he was born and died. In the past, we spoiled and polluted parts of that nature, inflicted environmental "damage." But that was like stabbing a man with toothpicks: though it hurt, annoyed, degraded, it did not touch vital organs, block the path of the lymph or blood. We never thought that we had wrecked nature. Deep down, we never really thought we could: it was too big and too old; its forces—the wind, the rain, the sun—were too strong, too elemental.

But, quite by accident, it turned out that the carbon dioxide and other gases we were producing in our pursuit of a better life—in pursuit of warm houses and eternal economic growth and of agriculture so productive it would free most of us from farming—*could* alter the power of the sun, could increase its heat. And that increase *could* change the patterns of moisture and dryness, breed storms in new places, breed deserts. Those things may or may not have yet begun to happen, but it is too late to altogether prevent them from happening. We have produced the carbon dioxide—we are ending nature.

We have not ended rainfall or sunlight; in fact, rainfall and sunlight may become more important forces in our lives. It is too early to tell exactly how much harder the wind will blow, how much hotter the sun will shine. That is for the future. But the *meaning* of the wind, the sun, the rain—of nature—has already changed. Yes, the wind still blows—but no longer from some other sphere, some inhuman place.

In the summer, my wife and I bike down to the lake nearly every afternoon for a swim. It is a dogleg Adirondack lake, with three beaver lodges, a blue heron, some otter, a family of mergansers, the occasional loon. A few summer houses cluster at one end, but mostly it is surrounded by wild state land. During the week we swim across and back, a trip of maybe forty minutes—plenty of time to forget everything but the feel of the water around your body and the rippling, muscular joy of a hard kick and the pull of your arms.

But on the weekends, more and more often, someone will bring a boat out for waterskiing, and make pass after pass up and down the lake. And then the whole experience changes, changes entirely. Instead of being able to forget everything but yourself, and even yourself except for the muscles and the skin, you must be alert, looking up every dozen strokes to see where the boat is, thinking about what you will do if it comes near. It is not so much the danger—few swimmers, I imagine, ever die by Evinrude. It's not even so much the blue smoke that hangs low over the water. It's that the motorboat gets in your mind. You're forced to think, not feel—to think of human society and of people. The lake is utterly different on these days, just as the planet is utterly different now.

THE ARGUMENT that nature is ended is complex; profound objections to it are possible, and I will try to answer them. But to understand what's ending requires some attention to the past. Not the ancient past, not the big bang or the primal stew. The European exploration of this continent is far enough back, for it is man's *idea* of nature that is important here, and it was in response to this wild new world that much of our modern notion of nature developed. North America, of course, was not entirely unaltered by man when the colonists arrived, but its previous occupants had treated it fairly well. In many places, it was wilderness.

And most of it was wilderness still on the eve of the Revolution, when William Bartram, one of America's first professional naturalists, set out from his native Philadelphia to tour the South. His report on that trip through "North and South Carolina, Georgia, East and West Florida, the Cherokee Country, the Extensive Territories of the Muscogulges, or Creek Confederacy, and the Country of the Choctaws" is a classic; it gives the sharpest early picture of this fresh continent. Though some of the land he traveled had been settled (he spent a number of his nights with gentlemen farmers on their plantations), the settlement was sparse, and the fields of indigo and rice gave way quickly to the wilderness. And not the dark and forbidding wilderness of European fairy tales but a blooming, humming, fertile paradise. Every page of Bartram's long journal shouts of the fecundity, the profligacy, of this fresh land. "I continued several miles [reaching] verdant swelling knolls, profusely productive of flowers and fragrant strawberries, their rich juice dyeing my horse's feet and ankles." When he stops for dinner, he catches a trout, picks a wild orange, and stews the first in the juices of the second over his fire.

Whatever direction he struck off in, Bartram found vigorous beauty. He could not even stumble in this New World without discovering something: near the Broad River, while ascending a "steep, rocky hill," he slips and reaching for a shrub to steady himself he tears up several plants of a new species of *Caryophyllata (geum odoratissimum)*. Fittingly, their roots "filled the air with animating scents of cloves and spicy perfumes." His diary brims over with the grand Latin binomials of a thousand plants and animals—*Kalmia latifolia*, "snowy mantled" *Philadelphus inodorus, Pinus sylvestris, Populus tremula, Dionea muscipula* ("admirable are the properties" of these "sportive vegetables"!), *Rheum rhubarbarum, Magnolia grandiflora*— and also with the warm common names: the bank martin, the water wagtail, the mountain cock, the chattering plover, the bumblebee. But the roll call of his adjectives is even more indicative of his mood. On one page, in the account of a single afternoon, he musters fruitful, fragrant, sylvan (twice), moderately warm, exceedingly pleasant, charming, fine, joyful, most beautiful, pale gold, golden, russet, silver (twice), blue green, velvet black, orange, prodigious, gilded, delicious, harmonious, soothing, tuneful, sprightly, elevated, cheerful (twice), high and airy, brisk and cool, clear, moonlit, sweet, and healthy. Even where he can't see, he imagines marvels: the fish disappearing into subterranean streams, "where, probably, they are separated from each other by innumerable paths, or secret rocky avenues, and after encountering various obstacles, and beholding new and unthought-of scenes of pleasure and disgust, after many days' absence from the surface of the world emerge again from the dreary vaults, and appear exulting in gladness and sporting in the transparent waters of some far distant lake." But he is no Disney—this is no *Fantasia*. He is a scientist recording his observations, and words like "cheerful" and "sweet" seem to have been technical descriptions of the untouched world in which he wandered.

This sort of joy in the natural was not a literary convention, a given; as Paul Brooks points out in *Speaking for Nature*, much of literature had regarded wilderness as ugly and crude until the Romantic movement of the late eighteenth century. Andrew Marvell, for instance, referred to mountains as "ill-designed excrescences." This silliness changed into a new silliness with the Romantics; Chateaubriand's immensely popular *Atala*, for instance, describes the American wilderness as filled with bears "drunk with grapes, and reeling on the branches of the elm trees." But the rapturous fever took on a healthier aspect in this country. If most of the pioneers, to be sure, saw a buffalo as something to hunt, a forest as something to cut down, a flock of passenger pigeons as a call to heavy artillery (farmers would bring their hogs to feed on the carcasses of pigeons raining down in the slaughter), there were always a good many (even, or especially, among the hunters and loggers) who recognized and described the beauty and order of this early time.

Of a thousand examples, my favorite single description comes from George Catlin, who traveled across the frontier to paint the portraits of American Indians. In his journal he describes a night he spent while riding north from Fort Gibson to the Missouri River in order to escape an epidemic. His camp was "in one of the most lovely little valleys I ever saw, and even far more beautiful than could be imagined by mortal man," he writes, "an enchanting little lawn of five or six acres, on the banks of a cool and rippling stream, that was alive with fish; and every now and then, a fine brood of ducks, just old enough for delicious food and too unsophisticated to avoid an easy and simple death. This little lawn was surrounded by bunches and copses of the most picturesque foliage, consisting of lofty bois d'arcs and elms, spreading their huge branches as if offering protection to the rounded groups of cherry and plum trees that supported festoons of grapevines with their purple clusters that hung in the most tempting manner over the green carpet that was everywhere decked out with wild flowers of all tints and various sizes, from the modest wild sunflowers, with their thousand tall and droopy heads, to the lilies that stood, and the violets that crept, beneath them. . . . The wild deer were repeatedly rising from their quiet lairs, and bounding out and over the graceful swells of the prairies which hemmed it in." If this passage had a little number at the start of each sentence, it could be Genesis; it sticks in my mind as a baseline, a reminder of where we began.

SUCH VISIONS of the world as it existed outside human history became scarcer with each year that passed, of course. By the 1930s, when Bob Marshall, the founder of the Wilderness Society, set off to explore Alaska's Brooks Range, all the lower forty-eight states had been visited, mapped, and named. "Often, as when visiting Yosemite or Glacier Park or the Grand Canyon or Avalanche Lake or some other natural scene of surpassing beauty, I had wished self-ishly enough that I might have had the joy of being the first person to discover it," he wrote. "I had been thrilled reading Captain Lewis's glowing account of the great falls of the Missouri. I yearned for adventures comparable to those of Lewis and Clark." And he found them, on the upper reaches of the Koyukuk River, where no one, not even an Alaskan Eskimo, seems ever to have been before. Each day brought eight, ten, a dozen ridges and streams and peaks under his eye and hence into human history. One morning he came around a corner to discover that "the Clear River emerged from none of three gorges we had imagined, but from a hidden valley which turned almost at right angles to the west. I cannot convey in words my feeling in finding this broad valley lying there, just as fresh and untrammeled as at the dawn of geological eras hundreds of millions of years ago. Nor is there any adequate way of describing the scenery. . . . I could make mention of thousand-foot sheer precipices; I could liken the valley to a Yosemite without waterfalls, but with rock domes beside which the world-renowned Half Dome would be trivial—yet with all that I would not have conveyed the sense of the continuous, exulting feeling of immensity. . . . Best of all it was fresh—gloriously fresh. At every step there was the exhila-rating feeling of breaking new ground. There were no musty signs of human occupation. This, beyond a doubt, was an unbeaten path."

Marshall was very near the last to see surroundings unpolluted even by the knowledge that someone had been there before.

Though his explorations were made not long before World War II, they were an anomaly, a last gasp of the voyages of discovery that marked an earlier epoch. It is hard for us to credit that only a hundred and twenty years ago the valley of the Colorado—the Grand Canyon—was a blank spot on maps of the Southwest, or that sixty years before that the Rockies were a rumor among white men. That when Thoreau climbed Maine's Mt. Katahdin in 1846 he could list the names of the five Europeans who had preceded him up the peak. "I am reminded by my journey how exceedingly new this country is," Thoreau wrote. "Those Maine woods differ essentially from ours [in Concord, Massachusetts]. There you are never reminded that the wilderness which you are threading is, after all, some villager's familiar wood-lot, some widow's thirds, from which her ancestors have sledded fuel for generations, minutely described in some old deed." Here in the Adirondacks, our highest peak, Mt. Marcy, was not climbed by a white man until 1837, a generation after the return of Lewis and Clark.

We are rarely reminded anymore of the continent's newness. That era of discovery is as firmly closed to us as the age of knights and dragons. Katahdin, though preserved as a park, is so popular that the authorities must strictly limit the number of campers— some days hundreds are at the summit simultaneously. The trail up Mt. Marcy on a holiday weekend is like the Macy's escalators with a heavy balsam scent. I once interviewed a man who was *rowing* to Antarctica from Tierra del Fuego because, he explained, "you can't be the first to explore the blank spots on the map or to climb the mountains anymore. It has a lot more to do with style now." (He had previously skied *around* Mt. Everest.) Not even the moon to conquer!

Over time, though, we've reconciled ourselves to the idea that we'll not be the first up any hill, and, indeed, we've come to appreciate the history of a spot as a source of added pleasure and interest. On the prairies we search for the rutted tracks left by the wagon trains; at Walden Pond, where Thoreau sought to escape man, we dutifully trek around the shore to see the site of his cabin. In something of the same fashion, we have come to accept, and enjoy, the intrusion of scientific explanation—to know that we can marvel with undiminished awe at the south wall of the Grand Canyon even while understanding the geologic forces that carved it. The Grand Canyon is so . . . grand that we can cope with not being the first people to see it. The wonder of nature does not depend on its freshness.

BUT STILL WE FEEL the need for pristine places, places substantially *unaltered* by man. Even if we do not visit them, they matter to us. We need to know that though we are surrounded by buildings there are vast places where the world goes on as it always has. The Arctic National Wildlife Refuge, on Alaska's northern shore, is reached by just a few hundred people a year, but it has a vivid life in the minds of many more, who are upset that oil companies want to drill there. And upset not only because it may or may not harm the caribou but because here is a vast space free of roads and buildings and antennas, a blank spot if not on the map then on the surface. It sickens us to hear that "improper waste disposal practices" at the American Antarctic research station in McMurdo Sound have likely spread toxic waste on that remote continent, or that an Exxon tanker has foundered off the port of Valdez, tarring the beaches with petroleum.

One proof of the deep-rooted desire for pristine places is the decision that Americans and others have made to legislate "wilderness"—to set aside vast tracts of land where, in the words of the federal statute, "the earth and its community of life are untrammeled by man, where man himself is a visitor who does not remain." Pristine nature, we recognize, has been overwhelmed in many places, even in many of our national parks. But in these few spots it makes a stand. If we can't have places where no man has ever been, we can at least have spots where no man is at the moment.

Segregating such wilderness areas has not been easy. The quiet of the land behind my house, fifty thousand acres of state wilderness, is daily broken by Air Force jets practicing flying beneath radar; they come in pairs, twisting and screeching above the hills, so that for a moment, and a few moments after that, it is no wilderness at all. And often, of course, man invades more insidiously: the synthetic compounds of man's pesticides, for instance, worm their way slowly but inevitably into the fabric of life.

But, even under such stress, it is still wilderness, still pristine in our minds. Most of the day, the sky above my mountain is simply sky, not "airspace." Standing in the middle of a grimy English mill town, George Orwell records this "encouraging" thought: "In spite of hard trying, man has not yet succeeded in doing his dirt everywhere. The earth is so vast and still so empty that even in the filthy heart of civilization you find fields where the grass is green instead of grey; perhaps if you looked for them you might even find streams with live fish in them instead of salmon tins." When Rachel Carson wrote *Silent Spring*, she was able to find some parts of the Arctic still untouched—no DDT in the fish, the beaver, the beluga, the caribou, the moose, the polar bear, the walrus. The cranberries, the strawberries, and the wild rhubarb all tested clean, though two snowy owls, probably as a result of their migrations, carried small amounts of the pesticide, as did the livers of two Eskimos who had been away to the hospital in Anchorage.

In other words, as pervasive a problem as DDT was, and is, one could, and can, always imagine that *somewhere* a place existed free of its taint. (And largely as a result of Carson's book there are more and more such places.) As pervasive and growing as the problem of acid rain surely is, at the moment places still exist with a rainfall of an acceptable, "normal" pH. And if we wished to stop acid rain we could; experimenters have placed tents over groves of trees to demonstrate that if the acid bath ceases, a forest will return to normal. Even the radiation from an event as nearly universal as the explosion at the Chernobyl plant has begun to fade, and Scandinavians can once more eat their vegetables.

We can, in other words, still plausibly imagine wild nature—or, at least, the possibility of wild nature in the future—in all sorts of places.

This idea of nature is hardy. Our ability to shut the destroyed areas from our minds, to see beauty around man's degradation, is considerable. A few years ago I spent some days driving around Arizona in a van with a man named Lyn Jacobs, one of a small number of environmentalists fighting a difficult battle to restrict the grazing of cattle on public lands in the West. The cows, which range over 70 percent of the federal land in the American West under a leasing program that does not pay for itself and each year requires tax subsidies, produce about 3 percent of America's beef. And by their constant grazing, the cattle convert the rangelands into barren pastures. Where there are streams they cave in the banks; where there are wildfowl they trample their nests. In their wake they leave stands of cheatgrass and thistle in place of the natural long-stemmed grasses. But the West has been a pasture so long that practically no one notices. People just assume that grass there can't grow more than a foot high. One morning, Jacobs and I drove along a ranch road that ran just parallel to the Grand Canyon about fifteen miles from the south rim. It was a glorious day, the sky a polarized blue, and though you couldn't see the canyon you knew with heart-stopping precision where it was, for the clouds dropped over its edge, their bottoms obscured like icebergs. "That's the problem," Jacobs said, stopping the van. "When you look at Western panoramas, you don't look down—your eye is trained to think this desert is normal. You tend to look at the mountains and the blue sky above them, and the clouds."

The idea of wildness, in other words, can survive most of the "normal" destruction of nature. Wildness can survive in our minds once the land has been discovered and mapped and even chewed up. It can survive all sorts of pollution, even the ceaseless munching of a million cows. If the ground is dusty and trodden, we look at the sky; if the sky is smoggy, we travel someplace where it's clear; if we can't travel to someplace where it's clear, we *imagine* ourselves in Alaska or Australia or some place where it is, and that works nearly as well. Nature, while often fragile in reality, is durable in our imaginations. Wildness, the idea of wildness, has outlasted the exploration of the entire globe. It has endured the pesticides and the pollution. When the nature around us is degraded, we picture it fresh and untainted elsewhere. When elsewhere, too, it rains acid or DDT, we can still imagine that someday soon it will be better, that we will stop polluting and despoiling and instead "restore" nature. (And, indeed, people have begun to do just this sort of work: here in the Adirondacks, helicopters drop huge quantities of lime into lakes in order to reduce their acidity.) In our minds, nature suffers from a terrible case of acne, or even skin cancer—but our faith in its essential strength remains, for the damage always seems local.

BUT NOW THE BASIS of that faith is lost. The idea of nature will not survive the new global pollution—the carbon dioxide and the CFCs and the like. This new rupture with nature is different not only in scope but also in kind from salmon tins in an English stream. We have changed the atmosphere, and thus we are changing the weather. By changing the weather, we make every spot on earth man made and artificial. We have deprived nature of its independence, and that is fatal to its meaning. Nature's independence *is* its meaning; without it there is nothing but us.

If you travel by plane and dog team and snowshoe to the farthest corner of the Arctic and it is a mild summer day, you will not know whether the temperature is what it is "supposed" to be, or whether, thanks to the extra carbon dioxide, you are standing in the equivalent of a heated room. If it is twenty below and the wind is howling—perhaps absent man it would be forty below. Since most of us get to the North Pole only in our minds, the real situation is more like this: if in July there's a heat wave in London, it won't be a natural phenomenon. It will be a man-made phenomenon—an amplification of what nature intended or a total invention. Or, at the very least, it *might* be a man-made phenomenon, which amounts to the same thing. The storm that might have snapped the hot spell may never form, or may veer off in some other direction, not by the laws of nature but by the laws of nature as they have been rewritten, blindly, crudely, but effectively, by man. If the sun is beating down on you, you will not have the comfort of saying, "Well, that's nature." Or if the sun feels sweet on the back of your neck, that's fine, but it isn't nature. A child born now will never know a natural summer, a natural autumn, winter, or spring. Summer is going extinct, replaced by something else that will be called "summer." This new summer will retain some of its relative characteristics—it will be hotter than the rest of the year, for instance, and the time of year when crops grow—but it will not be summer, just as even the best prosthesis is not a leg.

And, of course, climate determines an enormous amount of the rest of nature—where the forests stop and the prairies or the tundra begins, where the rain falls and where the arid deserts squat, where the wind blows strong and steady, where the glaciers form, how fast the lakes evaporate, where the seas rise. As John Hoffman, of the Environmental Protection Agency, noted in the *Journal of Forestry*, "trees planted today will be entering their period of greatest growth when the climate has already changed." A child born today might swim in a stream free of toxic waste, but he won't ever see a natural stream. If the waves crash up against the beach, eroding dunes and destroying homes, it is not the awesome power of Mother Nature. It is the awesome power of Mother Nature as altered by the awesome power of man, who has overpowered in a century the processes that have been slowly evolving and changing of their own accord since the earth was born.

Those "record highs" and "record lows" that the weathermen are always talking about—they're meaningless now. It's like comparing pole vaults between athletes using bamboo and those using fiberglass poles, or dash times between athletes who've been chewing steroids and those who've stuck to Wheaties. They imply a connection between the past and the present which doesn't exist. The comparison is like hanging Rembrandts next to Warhols; we live in a postnatural world. Thoreau once said he could walk for half an hour and come to "some portion of the earth's surface where man does not stand from one year's end to another, and there, consequently, politics are not, for they are but the cigar-smoke of a man." Now you could walk half a year and not reach such a spot. Politics—our particular way of life, our ideas about how we should live—now blows its smoke over every inch of the globe.

About a half mile from my house, right at the head of the lake, the town has installed a streetlight. It is the only one for miles, and it is undeniably useful—without it, a car or two each summer would undoubtedly miss the turn and end up in the drink. Still, it intrudes on the dark. Most of the year, once the summer people have left, there is not another light to be seen. On a starry night the Milky Way stands out like a marquee; on a cloudy night you can walk in utter pitch black, unable to see even the dog trotting at your side. But then, around the corner, there is the streetlamp, and soon you are in its sodium-vapor circle, a circle robbed of mystery by its illumination. It's true that the bugs love the lamp; on a June night there is more wildlife buzzing around it than in any square acre of virgin forest. But it breaks up the feeling of the night. And now it is as if we had put a huge lamp in the sky, and cast that same prosaic sterile light at all times on all places.

WHILE I WAS stacking wood one morning last fall I noticed a lot of ash floating through the air. "Did you make a fire?" I asked my wife through the window. "No," she said. I wandered off down the road to see if it was coming from the nearest occupied house—but that's quite a way off. I finally stopped long enough to trap a piece of the ash in my fist so I could look at it. It turned out to be a bug I had never seen before—a blackflylike creature with a gray, woolly clump of something on its back that certainly looked like ash. Not man! Nature!

If only that were the case with most of the changes around us—if only all the analogies were just analogies. If only they were all figments, and the world were the same old place it had always been. But the world, the whole world, is touched by our work, even when that work is invisible.

In a famous essay, "Sootfall and Fallout," which was written at the height of the atmospheric atomic testing in the early 1960s, E. B. White says that the joy he always took in his newly dug garden patch "has been spoiled by the maggots that work in the mind. Tomorrow we will have rain, and the rain falling on the garden will carry its cargo of debris from old explosions in distant places. Whether the amount of this freight is great or small, whether it is measurable by the farmer or can only be guessed at, one thing is certain: the character of rain has changed, the joy of watching it soak the waiting earth has been diminished, and the whole meaning and worth of gardens has been called into question." Happily, we have ceased atmospheric atomic testing. Unhappily, White's words still hold true; only now the culprits—carbon dioxide, methane, nitrous oxide, chlorofluorocarbons—are the result not of some high and distant drama, a few grand explosions, but of a billion explosions of a hundred million pistons every second, near and far and insidiously common.

We will have a hard time believing this new state of affairs. Even the most farseeing naturalists of an earlier day couldn't comprehend that the atmosphere, the climate, could be dramatically altered. Thoreau, complaining about the logging that eventually destroyed virtually every stand of virgin timber between the Atlantic and the Mississippi, said that soon the East "would be so bald that every man would have to grow whiskers to hide its nakedness, but, thank God, the sky was safe." And John Muir, the Scottish-born explorer of Yosemite, wrote one day in his diary about following a herd of grazing sheep through the valley: "Thousands of feet trampling leaves and flowers, but in this mighty wilderness they seem but a feeble band, and a thousand gardens should escape their blighting touch. They cannot hurt the trees, though some of the seedlings suffer, and should the woolly locusts be greatly multiplied, as on account of dollar value they are likely to be, then the forests too, in time, may be destroyed. Only the sky will then be safe." George Perkins Marsh, the first modern environmentalist, knew a century ago that cutting down forests was a horrible idea, yet he said, "The revolutions of the seasons, with their alterations of temperatures, and of length of day and night, the climate of different zones, and the general conditions and movements of the atmosphere and seas, depend upon causes for the most part cosmical, and, of course, beyond our control."

And even as it dawns on us what we have done, there will be plenty of opportunity to forget, at least for a while, that anything has changed. For it isn't natural *beauty* that is ended; in fact, in the same way that the smog breeds spectacular sunsets, there may appear new, unimagined beauties. What will change is the meaning that beauty carries, for when we look at a sunset, we see, or think we see, many things beyond a particular arrangement of orange and purple and rose.

IT IS ALSO TRUE that this is not the first huge rupture in the globe's history. Perhaps thirty times since the earth formed, planetesimals up to ten miles in diameter and traveling at sixty times the speed of sound have crashed into the earth, releasing, according to the British scientist James Lovelock, perhaps a thousand times as much energy as would be liberated by the explosion of all present stocks of nuclear weapons. Such events, some scientists say, may have destroyed 90 percent of all living organisms. On an even larger scale, the sun has steadily increased its brightness; it has grown nearly 30 percent more luminous since life on earth began, forcing that life to keep forever scrambling to stay ahead—a race it will eventually lose, though perhaps not for some billions of years. Or consider an example more closely resembling the sharp divide we have now crossed. About two billion years ago, the microbiologist Lynn Margulis writes, the spread of certain sorts of bacteria caused, in short order, an increase in atmospheric oxygen from one part in a million to one part in just five—from 0.0001 percent to 21 percent. Compared to that, the increase in carbon dioxide from 280 to 560 parts per million is as the hill behind my house to Annapurna. "This was by far the greatest pollution crisis the earth has ever endured," Margulis writes. Oxygen poisoned most microbial life, which "had no defense against this cataclysm except the standard way of DNA replication and duplication, gene transfer and mutation." And, indeed, these produced the successful oxygen-synthesizing life forms that now dominate the earth.

But each of these examples is different from what we now experience, for they were "natural," as opposed to man made. A pint-size planet cracks into the earth; the ice advances; the sun, by the immutable laws of stars, burns brighter till its inevitable explosion; genetic mutation sets certain bacteria to spewing out oxygen and soon they dominate the planet, a "strictly natural" pollution.

One can, of course, argue that the current crisis, too, is "natural," because man is part of nature. This echoes the views of the earliest Greek philosophers, who saw no difference between matter and consciousness—nature included everything. James Lovelock wrote some years ago that "our species with its technology is simply an inevitable part of the natural scene," nothing more than mechanically advanced beavers. In this view, to say that we "ended" nature, or even damaged nature, makes no sense, since we *are* nature, and nothing we can do is "unnatural." This view can be, and is, carried to even greater lengths; Lynn Margulis, for instance, ponders the question of whether robots can be said to be living creatures, since any "invention of human beings is ultimately based on a variety of processes including that of DNA replication, no matter the separation in space or time of that replication from the invention."

But one can argue this forever and still not really feel it. It is a debater's point, a semantic argument. When I say that we have ended nature, I don't mean, obviously, that natural processes have ceased—there is still sunshine and still wind, still growth, still decay. Photosynthesis continues, as does respiration. *But we have ended the thing that has, at least in modern times, defined nature for us—its separation from human society.*

That separation is quite real. It is fine to argue, as certain poets and biologists have, that we must learn to fit in with nature, to recognize that we are but one species among many, and so on. But none of us, on the inside, quite believe it. The Sophists contrasted the "natural" with the "conventional"—what exists originally with what it becomes as the result of human intervention. And their distinction, filtered through Plato and Christianity and a dozen other screens, survives, because it agrees with our instinctive sense of the world. I sit writing here in my office. On the wall facing me there is a shelf of reference books—dictionaries, the *Guinness Book of Records*, a set of encyclopedias—and a typewriter and a computer. There's another shelf of books, all dealing with American history, on my left, and, on my right, pictures of my family, a stack of mail-order catalogs for Christmas shopping, and a radio broadcasting a Cleveland performance of Ravel's Piano Concerto in D for the left hand. Visible through the window is a steep mountain with nearly a mile of bare ridge and a pond almost at the peak.

The mountain and the office are separate parts of my life; I do not really think of them as connected. At night it's dark out there;

save for the streetlamp by the lake there's not a light for twenty miles to the west and thirty to the south. But in here the light shines. Its beams stretch a few yards into the night and then falter, turn to shadow, then black. In the winter it's cold out there, but in here the fire warms us until near dawn, and when it dwindles the oil burner kicks in.

What happens in here I control; what happens out there has always been the work of some independent force. That is not to say that the outside world isn't vitally important; I moved here so I could get to the mountains easily, and I think nature means a good deal even to the most inured city dweller. But it is enough for now to say that in our modern minds nature and human society are separate things. It is this separate nature I am talking about when I use the word—"nature," if you like.

One could also argue that we destroyed this independent nature long ago, that there's no present need for particular distress. That the day man made his first tool he irrevocably altered nature, or the day he planted his first crop. Walter Truett Anderson, in his recent book *To Govern Evolution*, makes the case that everything people do—including our attempts to set aside wilderness or protect endangered species—is "one way or another human intervention." California, his home, was permanently changed by the 1870s, he contends, when early agribusiness followed gold miners and shepherds. Technically, of course, he is correct. Any action alters its environment—even a bird building a nest—and it is true that we cannot, as he puts it, "return to a natural order untouched by human society." But Anderson's argument, and others like it that have often been employed as a rationale for further altering the environment, is too broad. Independent nature was not dead in California in 1870; in 1870, John Muir was just beginning his sojourn in Yosemite that would yield some of the greatest hymns to and insights into that world beyond man. As long as some places remained free and wild, the idea of the free and wild could live.

THE INVENTION of nuclear weapons may actually have marked the beginning of the end of nature: we possessed, finally, the capacity to overmaster nature, to leave an indelible imprint everywhere all at once. "The nuclear peril is usually seen in isolation from the threats to other forms of life and their ecosystems, but in fact it should be seen at the very center of the ecological crisis, as the cloud-covered Everest of which the more immediate, visible kinds of harm to the environment are the mere foothills," wrote Jonathan Schell in *The Fate of the Earth*. And he was correct, for at the time he was writing (less than a decade ago!) it was hard to conceive of any threats of the same magnitude. Global warming was one obscure theory among many. Nuclear weapons were unique (and they remain so, if only for the speed with which they work). But the nuclear dilemma is at least open to human reason—we can decide not to drop the weapons, and indeed to reduce and perhaps eliminate them. And the horrible power of these weapons, which has been amply demonstrated in Japan and on Bikini and under Nevada and many times in our imaginations, has led us fitfully in that hopeful direction.

By contrast, the various processes that lead to the end of nature have been essentially beyond human thought. Only a few people knew that carbon dioxide would warm up the world, for instance, and they were for a long time unsuccessful in their efforts to alert the rest of us. Now it is too late—not too late, as I shall come to explain, to ameliorate some of the changes and so perhaps to avoid the most gruesome of their consequences. But the scientists agree that we have already pumped enough gas into the air so that a significant rise in temperature and a subsequent shift in weather are inevitable.

Just how inevitable we can see from the remedies that some scientists have proposed to save us—not the remedies, like cutting fossil fuel use and saving the rain forests, that will keep things from being any worse than they need to be, but the solutions that might bring things back to "normal." The most natural method anyone has suggested involves growing enormous numbers of trees to take the carbon dioxide out of the air. Take, for argument's sake, a new coal-fired electric generating station that produces a thousand megawatts and operates at 38 percent thermal efficiency and 70 percent availability. To counteract just the carbon dioxide generated by that plant, the surrounding area to a radius of 24.7 kilometers would need to be covered with American sycamore trees (a fast-growing species) planted at four-foot intervals and "harvested" every four years. It might be possible to achieve that sort of growth rate—a government forestries expert told the Senate that with genetic screening, spacing, thinning, pruning, weed control, fire and pest control, fertilization, and irrigation, net annual growth could be "very much higher than at present." Even if it worked, though, would this tree plantation be nature? A walk through an endless glade of evenly spaced sycamores, with the weed-control chopper hovering overhead, and the irrigation pipes gurgling quietly below, represents a fundamental break with my idea of the wild world.

Other proposals get even odder. One "futuristic idea" described in *The New York Times* springs from the brain of Dr. Thomas Stix at Princeton: he proposes the possibility of using a laser to "scrub" chlorofluorocarbons from the earth's atmosphere before they have a chance to reach the ozone layer. Dr. Stix calculates that an array of infrared lasers spaced around the world could "blast apart" a million tons of chlorofluorocarbons a year—a procedure he refers to as "atmospheric processing." Down at the University of Alabama, Leon Y. Sadler, a chemical engineer, has suggested employing dozens of airplanes to carry ozone into the stratosphere (others have suggested firing a continuous barrage of "bullets" of frozen ozone, which would melt in the stratosphere). To deal with the warming problem, Columbia geochemist Wallace Broecker has considered a "fleet of several hundred jumbo jets" to ferry 35 million tons of sulfur dioxide into the stratosphere annually to reflect sunlight away from the earth. Other scientists recommend launching "giant orbiting satellites made of thin films" that could cast shadows on the earth, counteracting the greenhouse effect with a sort of venetian-blind effect. Certain practical problems may hamper these various solutions; Dr. Broecker, for instance, admits that injecting large quantities of sulfur dioxide into the atmosphere would increase acid rain "and give the blue sky a whitish cast." Still, they just might work. And perhaps, as Dr. Broecker contends, "a rational society needs some sort of insurance policy on how to maintain a habitable planet." But even if they do work—even if the planet remains habitable—it will not be the same. The whitish afternoon sky blessed by the geometric edge of the satellite cloud will fade into a dusk crisscrossed by lasers. There is no way to reassemble nature—certainly not by following the suggestion of one researcher that, in order to increase the earth's reflectivity and thus cool its temperature, we should cover most of the oceans with a floating layer of white Styrofoam chips.

There are some people, perhaps many, to whom this rupture will mean little. A couple of years ago a group of executives went rafting down a river in British Columbia; after an accident killed five of them, one of the survivors told reporters that the party had regarded the river as "a sort of ersatz roller-coaster." Nature has become a hobby with us. One person enjoys the outdoors, another likes cooking, a third favors breaking into military computers over his phone line. The nature hobby boomed during the 1970s; now it is perhaps in slight decline (the number of people requesting permits to hike and camp in the rugged backcountry of the national parks has dropped by half since 1983, even as the number of drive-through visitors has continued to increase). We have become in rapid order a people whose conscious need for nature is superficial. The seasons don't matter to most of us anymore except as spectacles. In my county and in many places around this part of the nation, the fair that once marked the harvest now takes place in late August, while tourist dollars are still in heavy circulation. Why celebrate the harvest when you harvest every week with a shopping cart? I am a child of the suburbs, and even though I live on the edge of the wild I have only a tenuous understanding of the natural world. I can drive past hundreds of miles of fields without ever being able to figure out what's growing in them, unless it's corn. And even farmers have a lessened feel for the world around them. The essayist Wendell Berry quotes from an advertisement for a new tractor: "Outside—dust, noise, heat, storm, fumes. Inside—all is quiet, comfortable, safe. . . . Driver dials 'inside weather' to his liking. . . . He pushbuttons radio or stereo-tape entertainment."

Even this is several steps above the philosophy expressed by a mausoleum director in a full-page newspaper ad that seems to run once a week in my newspaper: "Above-Ground. The Clean Burial.

Not Underground with Earth's Disturbing Elements." Four of his "clean, dry, civilized" vaults are already sold out, and a fifth is under construction. While we are still alive, we do sometimes watch a nature program, an account of squid or wildebeest, usually sponsored by Mutual of Omaha. Mostly, however, we watch *L.A. Law*.

STILL, THE PASSING of nature as we have known it, like the passing of any large idea, will have its recognizable effects, both immediately and over time. In 1893, when Frederick Jackson Turner announced to the American Historical Association that the frontier was closed, no one was aware that the frontier had been the defining force in American life. But in its absence it was understood. One reason we pay so little close attention to the separate natural world around us is that it has always been there and we presumed it always would. As it disappears, its primal importance will be clearer—in the same way that some people think they have put their parents out of their lives and learn differently only when the day comes to bury them.

How will we feel the end of nature? In many ways, I suspect. If nature means Bartram's great joy at fresh and untrammeled beauty, its loss means sadness at man's footprints everywhere. But, as with the death of a person, there is more than simply loss, a hole opening up. There are also new relationships that develop, and strains and twists in old relationships. And since this loss is peculiar in not having been inevitable, it provokes profound questions that don't arise when a person dies.

The first of these questions, I think, has to do with God. It may seem odd to take a physical event and go straight to the metaphysical for its meaning. But, as we have seen, nature is as much an idea as a fact. And in some way that idea is connected with God. I hesitate to go further than that, for I am no theologian; I am not even certain what I mean by God. (Perhaps some theologians join me in this difficulty.)

It is not a novel observation that religion has been in decline in the modern era. Despite the recent rise of fundamentalism, the crisis of belief continues. Many people, including me, have overcome it to a greater or a lesser degree by locating God in nature. Most of the glimpses of immortality, design, and benevolence that I see come from the natural world—from the seasons, from the beauty, from the intermeshed fabric of decay and life, and so on. Other signs exist as well, such as instances of great and selfless love between people, but these, perhaps, are less reliable. They hint at epiphany, not at the eternity that nature proclaimed. If this seems a banal notion, that is exactly my point. The earliest gods we know about were animals—tigers, birds, fish. Their forms and faces peer out from ancient ruins, and from the totems and wall paintings of our first religions.

And though, as time went on, we began to give our gods human features, much feeling still adheres to the forests and fields and birds and lions—else why should we moan about the "desecration" of our environment? I am a reasonably orthodox Methodist, and I go to church on Sunday because fellowship matters, because I find meaning in the history of the Israelites and in the Gospels, and because I love to sing hymns. But it is not in "God's house" that I feel his presence most—it is in his outdoors, on some sun-warmed slope of pine needles or by the surf. It is there that the numbing categories men have devised to contain this mystery—sin and redemption and incarnation and so on—fall away, leaving the overwhelming sense of the goodness and the sweetness at work in the world.

Perhaps this emotion has dimmed in an urban age, and most people now perceive God through the Christian Broadcasting Network. There is no question, though, that this is one thing nature *has* meant, and meant not just to the ancients but to the great American naturalists who first helped us see the outdoor world as more than a source of raw materials or the home of dangerous animals. "We now use the word Nature very much as our fathers used the word God," John Burroughs wrote at the turn of the century, "and, I suppose, back of it all we mean the power that is everywhere present and active, and in whose lap the visible universe is held and nourished." There are, he added, "no atheists and skeptics in regard to this knowledge." Nature is reality, Thoreau said—distinct from the "Arabian nights entertainments" that humans concoct for themselves. "God himself culminates in the present moment, and will never be more divine in the lapse of all the ages. And we are enabled to apprehend at all what is sublime and noble only by the perpetual instilling and drenching of the reality that surrounds us." That drenching could come in the woods around Walden, but better in true wilderness. On his trip to Mt. Katahdin, Thoreau looked around at the uncut miles and said: "Perhaps where *our* wild pines stand and leaves lie on the forest floor in Concord, there were once reapers, and husband-men planted grain; but here not even the surface had been scarred by man. . . . It was a specimen of what God saw fit to make this world." The earth is a museum of divine intent.

Simply saying that we apprehend God in nature, however, is just a beginning. It may be true, as a mystic once contended, that most people, sometime in their lives, are moved by natural beauty to a "mood of heightened consciousness" in which "each blade of grass seems fierce with meaning," but the question is: What meaning? "All nature," contended another mystic a century ago, "is the language in which God expresses his thought." Very well, but what thought is that?

The chief lesson is that the world displays a lovely order, an order comforting in its intricacy. And the most appealing part of this harmony, perhaps, is its permanence—the sense that we are part of something with roots stretching back nearly forever, and branches reaching forward just as far. Purely human life provides only a partial fulfillment of this desire for a kind of immortality. As individuals, we can feel desperately alone: we may not have children, or we may not care much for how they have turned out; we may not care to trace ourselves back through our parents; some of us may even be general misanthropes, or feel that our lives are unimportant, brief, and hurried rushes toward a final emptiness. But the earth and all its processes—the sun growing plants, flesh feeding on these plants, flesh decaying to nourish more plants, to name just one cycle—gives us some sense of a more enduring role. The poet Robinson Jeffers, a deeply pessimistic man with regard to the human condition, once wrote, "The parts change and pass, or die, people and races and rocks and stars; none of them seems to me important in itself, but only the whole. . . . It seems to me that this whole alone is worthy of a deeper sort of love; and that there is peace, freedom, I might say a kind of salvation. . . ."

John Muir expressed this sense of immortality best. Born to a stern Calvinist father who used a belt to help him memorize the Bible, Muir eventually escaped to the woods, traveling to the Yosemite Valley of California's Sierra Nevada. The journal of his first summer there is filled with a breathless joy at the beauty around him. Again and again in that Sierra June, "the greatest of all the months of my life," he uses the word "immortality," and he uses it in a specific way, designed to contrast with his father's grim and selfish religion. Time ceases to have its normal meaning in those hills: "Another glorious Sierra day in which one seems to be dissolved and sent pulsing onward we know not where. Life seems neither long nor short, and we take no more heed to save time or make haste than do the trees and stars. This is true freedom, a good practical sort of immortality." In a mood like this, space is no more imposing a boundary than time: "We are now in the mountains, and they are now in us, making every nerve quiet, filling every pore and cell of us. Our flesh-and-bone tabernacle seems transparent as glass to the beauty around us, as if truly an inseparable part of it, thrilling with the air and trees, streams and rocks, in the waves of the sun—a part of all nature, neither old nor young, sick nor well, but immortal."

Still, moving as it is, all this remains slightly vague, transcendental. For Burroughs and for Muir and for Thoreau, God didn't have a name or a doctrine. For many of us in the West this fuzzy notion of God is all there is, just as for many others God is all too obvious in his likes and his dislikes. In fact, to the degree that our dominant Judeo-Christian tradition is seen as saying anything about nature, it is usually seen as anti-environmentalist, as elevating man above all others. The Genesis story, with its emphasis upon dominion ("Fill the earth and subdue it, and have dominion over the fish of the sea and over the birds of the air and over every living thing that moves upon the earth"), appears the perfect rationale for cutting down forests, running roads through every wild place, killing off snail darters. The biblical tradition, Joseph Campbell says, is the "socially-oriented mythology" of a mobile people, as opposed to the nature-oriented mythology of an earth-cultivating society. Therefore, we control nature, or try to. In an influential essay written at the height of the environmental movement, Lynn White, Jr., said that Christianity bears "an immense burden of guilt" for the ecological crisis; to get some sense of his meaning requires only a trip to Utah, where the state motto is "Industry" and the Mormons have made a great project of subduing nature, erecting some towns in places so barren and dry and steep that only missionary zeal to conquer the wild could be the motivation.

But Christianity was long the bulwark of slavery, too; indeed, one could make at least as convincing an argument from the text that the Bible countenances chattel bondage as that it urges the rape of the land. Both rely on narrow readings of short passages; when the Bible is read as a whole, I think, the opposite messages resound, though we have been slow to hear them. For every passage like the one in Genesis there is a verse counseling moderation, love of land. In recent years, many theologians have contended that the Bible demands a careful "stewardship" of the planet instead of a careless subjugation, that immediately after giving man dominion over the earth God instructed him to "cultivate and keep it." But actually, I think, the Scriptures go much deeper. The Old Testament contains in many places, but especially in the book of Job, one of the most far-reaching defenses ever written of wilderness, of nature free from the hand of man. The argument gets at the heart of what the loss of nature will mean to us.

Job is, of course, the story of a just and prosperous man. The devil wagers God that Job's piety is merely a function of his success; bring him down and he will curse you, he says. God agrees to the bet, and soon Job is living on a dunghill on the edge of town, his flesh a mass of oozing sores, his children dead, his flock scattered, his property gone. He refuses to curse God, but he does demand a meeting with him and an explanation of his misfortune. Job refuses to accept the reasoning of his orthodox friends—that he has unknowingly sinned and is therefore being punished. Their view, that all the earth revolves around man, and every consequence is explained by man's action, doesn't satisfy Job: he knows he is innocent.

Finally, God arrives, a voice from the whirlwind. But instead of engaging in deep metaphysical discussion he talks at some length about nature, about concrete creation. "Where were you when I laid the earth's foundation?" he asks. In an exquisite poem he lists his accomplishments, his pride in his creation always evident. Was Job there when he "put the sea behind closed doors"? Job was not; therefore Job could not hope to understand many mysteries, including why rain falls "on land where no one lives, to meet the needs of the lonely wastes and make grass sprout upon the ground." God seems to be insisting that we are not the center of the universe, that he is quite happy if it rains where there are no people—that God is quite happy with *places* where there are no people, a radical departure from our most ingrained notions.

The end of the book contains descriptions of Behemoth and Leviathan, two creatures God has made and constrained. "Behold now Behemoth," booms God. "He eateth grass as an ox. Lo now, his strength is in his loins. And his force is in the muscles of his belly. He moveth his tail like a cedar. . . . His bones are as tubes of brass. His limbs are like bars of iron. . . . Behold, if a river overflow he trembleth not. He is confident, though Jordan swell even to his mouth. Shall any take him when he is on the watch, or pierce through his nose with a snare?" The answer, clearly, is no; the message, though not precisely an answer to Job's plaint, is that we may not judge everything from our point of view—that all nature is not ours to subdue.

There are some who have heard that message, even as most of the Western world has gone along its prideful way. Among the company of Christian saints, not one is more beloved than Francis of Assisi. We all have a mental image of him, usually that of a man in a brown robe whose shoulders and arms are covered with birds. His pastoral vision was not entirely unprecedented: for at least the first five centuries of the Church, the dominant Christian symbol had been Christ as the Good Shepherd instead of Christ on the Cross. And, granted, Francis's understanding of the importance of nature was somewhat different from ours—because water was used in baptism, says his biographer William Armstrong, Francis took pains not to tread where he had emptied his washbasin. But his essential idea was not baroque: just as God had sent Jesus to manifest him in human form, so too he represented himself in birds and flowers, streams and boulders, sun and moon, the sweetness of the air. Holding a small duck in his hand, wrote Bonaventure, Francis was in religious ecstasy: "He beheld in fair things Him who is the most fair."

Wild nature, then, has been a way to recognize God and to talk about who he is—even, as in Job, a way for God to talk about who he is. How could it be otherwise? What else is, or was, beyond human reach? In what other sphere could a deity operate freely? It is not chance that every second hymn in the hymn book rings with the imagery of the untouched outdoors. "All thy works with joy surround thee, Earth and Heaven reflect thy rays," we sing to Beethoven's "Ode to Joy." Sheep and harvests and the other common motifs of the Bible are not just metaphors; they are also the old reality of the earth, a place where people depended for both life and meaning on the nature they found around them. "We plow the fields and scatter the good seed on the land, But it is fed and watered by God's almighty hand. He sends the snow in winter, The warmth to swell the grain, The breezes and the sunshine, And soft refreshing rain. All good gifts around us Are sent from heaven above."

So what will the end of nature as we have known it mean to our understanding of God and of man? The important thing to remember is that the end of nature is not an impersonal event, like an earthquake. It is something we humans have brought about through a series of conscious and unconscious choices: *we* ended the natural atmosphere, and hence the natural climate, and hence the natural boundaries of the forests, and so on. In so doing, we exhibit a kind of power thought in the past to be divine (much as we do by genetically altering life).

We as a race turn out to be stronger than we suspected—much

stronger. In a sense we turn out to be God's equal—or, at least, his rival—able to destroy creation. This idea, of course, has been building for a while. "We became less and less capable of seeing ourselves as small within creation, partly because we thought we could comprehend it statistically, but also because we were becoming creators, ourselves, of a mechanical creation by which we felt ourselves greatly magnified," writes the essayist Wendell Berry. "Why, after all, should one get excited about a mountain when one can see almost as far from the top of a building, much farther from an airplane, farther still from a space capsule?" And our atomic weapons obviously created the *possibility* that we could exercise godlike powers.

But the possibility is different from the fact. We actually seem to have recognized the implications of nuclear weapons, and begun to back away from them—an unprecedented act of restraint. In our wholesale alteration of nature, though, we've shown no such timidity. And just as challenging one's parents and getting away with it rocks one's identity, so must this. Barry Lopez reports that the Yupik Eskimos refer to us Westerners "with incredulity and apprehension as 'the people who change nature.' " When changing nature means making a small modification in what we have found—a dam across a river—it presents few philosophical problems. (It presents some, especially when the river is a beautiful one, but they tend not to be ultimate problems.) When changing nature means changing everything, then we have a crisis. We are in charge now, like it or not. As a species we are as gods—our reach global.

And God has not stopped us. The possibilities—if there is or was any such thing as God, the eternal, the divine—include at least the following: God thoroughly approves of what we have done; it is our destiny. God doesn't approve, but is powerless to do anything about it, either because he is weak or because he has created us with free will. Or God is uninterested, or absent, or dead.

That last option is not a new formulation, of course. Nietzsche said some time ago that God was dead, and a lot of people began to agree with him after the Holocaust. The Holocaust and what I am calling the end of nature are not comparable events: the latter is an idea, like the closing of the frontier, and, at least for the moment, has less physical reality. But it may have similar faith-shattering effects. To many whose faith was built on God's covenant with the Israelites, on his promise to protect them, the Holocaust crushed belief or altered it enormously. For some Jewish thinkers, wrote the theologian Marc Ellis, "the Holocaust represents the severing of the relationship between God and person, God and community, God and culture. The lesson of the Holocaust is that humanity is alone and there is no meaning in life outside of human solidarity." (And human solidarity, of course, is eternally thrown into question by the Holocaust.) In a similar fashion, for those of us who have tended to locate God in nature—who, say, look upon spring as a sign of his existence and a clue to his meaning—what does it mean that we have destroyed the old spring and replaced it with a new one of our own devising? Why did he not stop us? Why did he allow it?

Perhaps it is all for the best, a break with some Druidic past. But it seems infinitely sad. And it seems to feed on itself, unlike the Holocaust, whose lessons maybe just possibly did increase the chances of human caring. How are we to be humble in any way if we have taken over as creators? Thoreau once stood in the woods watching "an insect crawling amid the pine needles on the forest floor, and endeavoring to conceal itself from my sight." It reminded him, he said (and Thoreau was not an especially humble man) of "the greater Benefactor and Intelligence that stands over me, the human insect." But what stands over us?

Religion will not end—far from it. We are probably in for a siege of apocalyptic and fanatic creeds. But a certain way of thinking about God—a certain language by which to describe the indescribable—will disappear. The stern God of Muir's father talked constantly of sin and condemnation, and in booming, angry tones. Muir's God spoke to him in the rush of water across the rocks and the cry of the jays around his camp. They were different Gods. "If we have a wonderful sense of the divine, it is because we live amid such awesome magnificence," wrote religious scholar Thomas Berry. "If we lived on the moon, our mind and emotions, our speech, our imagination, our sense of the divine would all reflect the desolation of the lunar landscape."

And even if we manage to control the physical effects of our actions—if we come to live in a planet-size park of magnificent scenery—our sense of the divine will change. It will be, at best, the difference between a zoo and a wilderness. The Bronx Zoo has done a wonderful job of exchanging cages for wide, grassy fields, but even though the antelope have room to get up to speed and the zebra wander as a striped herd, it never crosses your mind that you are actually in the bush instead of the Bronx. We live, all of a sudden, in an Astroturf world, and though an Astroturf world may have a God, he can't speak through the grass, or even be silent through it and let us hear.

"SCIENCE," OF COURSE, replaced "God" as a guiding concept for many people after Darwin. Or, really, the two were rolled up into a sticky ball. To some degree this was mindless worship of a miracle future, the pursuit of which has landed us in the fix we now inhabit. I was browsing the other day through a volume from the 1950s edited by the eminent astronomer Harlow Shapley. Called *A Treasury of Science*, it is filled with the wisdom of the ages, essays dating back to Hippocrates. But it also includes one example of the wisdom of our particular age, a thirteen-page treatise in which one Roger Adams forecasts the wonderful epoch ahead in *Man's Synthetic Future*. Chemists, he predicts, will replace natural products with "new, better, and cheaper compounds" of their own creation. "An official of the wool industry made a statement recently that the demand for wool as a fabric will never be replaced," Adams scoffs. "These words were spoken by one completely unfamiliar with the potentialities of chemical research." Leather, too: "With durable, moisture-absorbing plastics, the problem of synthetic shoe uppers will be solved." On and on he goes, through the wonders of DDT, the high hopes for chemicals that will "effectively kill the crabgrass in the bluegrass lawn," and a hundred other miracles. "Today life is mechanized, electrified, abundant, easy, because of the pushbutton era," he concludes. "In the future citizens will more effectively farm the land and the seas; obtain necessary minerals from the oceans; clothe themselves from the coal and oil . . . be cured of any ailments

by a variety of drugs and medicinals; be happy, healthy, and kittenish at a hundred years of age; and perhaps attend interplanetary
football matches in the Rose Bowl."

Not everyone who fell in love with science was such a glib
Dacron worshiper. An example, typical of a certain strain, was Donald Culross Peattie, a nature writer prominent in the years around
World War II. (Though his work has been largely forgotten, one of
his books, *An Almanac for Moderns,* was chosen by a book club as the
American volume written in the three years preceding 1940 that
was "most likely to become a classic.") Peattie defends the scientific
faith as fiercely as any man could: "What is the force, the discipline,
the brotherhood bound by vows to the pursuit of incorruptible
truth, which proves every step, is forever returning to verify, will
abandon any cherished tenet the moment it is not convincing?" he
asks. "What is it that works all the modern miracles, has put the
practicality into compassion for the suffering, has unchained men
from their superstitions, has endured persecution and martyrdom,
and still knows no fear?" Well, science, of course. But science is
only a method of getting at truth; it's the truth that matters. And
in Peattie's case, and in many others, the truth that emerged was—
nature.

Peattie lived at the moment when ecological understanding was
beginning to break through, and he found great comfort and safety
in the repeating patterns of nature, in the constant elements of the
periodic table that make up the earth and the stars. "If by 'supreme
command' I may express an order in nature that a man can understand and revere, then that command, that order, has always been
there. In fact, it is nature itself, revealed in science." Biologists, as-
tronomers, and physicists, "those who have looked most deeply,"
were the "surest, serenest" men that Peattie knew, because they
understood that "the immutable order of Nature is on our side. It is
on the side of life."

The hope that science could replace religion as a way for human
beings to cope with the world, then, was really a hope that "nature"
could replace "God" as a source of inspiration and understanding. Harmony, permanence, order, and an idea of our place in that
order—scientists searched for all that as diligently as Job, with their

unceasing attention to the "web of life" and the grand cycle of decay and rebirth. But nature, it turned out, was fragile: men could turn it on its head so that it was no longer "immutable" and no longer "on the side of life." The atom bomb proved that, by combining some of the elements in a new and interesting way that clearly held the possibility of wiping out most life. The useful ecological insight that, in Peattie's words, "it is even good to die, since death is a natural part of life" clearly didn't apply to atomic annihilation, nor, I think, does it apply to death in a world where the natural cycles have been so altered. What is a "natural part of life" in an unnatural world? How, if the seasons are no longer inevitable, can we accept the inevitability, and even the beauty, of death?

Scientists may argue that natural processes still rule—that the chemical reactions even now eating away the ozone or absorbing the earth's reflected heat are proof that nature is still in charge, still our master. And some physicists have always talked about God in the interstices of the atom, or in the mysteries of quantum theory, or, more recently, says Robert Wright, in his *Three Scientists and Their Gods*, in stitches of DNA and other bits of "information." To all but the few hundred people who really understand the math, though, this is a minor and secondhand comfort, an occult, esoteric knowledge. We draw our lessons from what we can see and feel and hear around us. The nature that matters is not the whirling fuzziness of electrons and quarks and neutrinos, which will continue unchanged; it is not the vast and strange worlds and fields and fluxes that scientists can find with their telescopes. The nature that matters is the temperature, and the rain, and the leaves turning color on the maples, and the raccoons around the garbage can.

We can no longer imagine that we are part of something larger than ourselves—that is what all this boils down to. We used to be. When we were only a few hundred million, or only a billion or two, and the atmosphere had the composition it would have had with or without us, then even Darwin's revelations could in the end only strengthen our sense of belonging to creation, and our wonder at the magnificence and abundance of that creation. And there was the possibility that something larger than us—Francis's God, Thoreau's Benefactor and Intelligence, Peattie's Supreme Command—reigned over us. We were as bears—we slept less, made better tools, took longer to rear our young, but we lived in a world that we found made for us, by God, or by physics and chemistry and biology, just as bears live in a world they find waiting for them. But now *we* make that world, affect its every operation (except a few—the alteration of day and night, the spin and wobble and path of the planet, the most elementary geologic and tectonic processes).

As a result, there is no one by our side. Bears are now a distinctly different order of being, creatures in our zoo, and they have to hope we can figure out a way for them to survive on our hot new planet. By domesticating the earth, even though we've done it badly, we've domesticated all that live on it. Bears hold more or less the same place now as golden retrievers. And there is nobody above us. God, who may or may not be acting in many other ways, is not controlling the earth. When he asks, as he does in Job, "Who shut in the sea with doors . . . and prescribed bounds for it?" and "Who can tilt the waterskins of the heavens?" we can now answer that it is us. Our actions will determine the level of the sea, and change the course and destination of every drop of precipitation. This is, I suppose, the victory we have been pointing to at least since the eviction from Eden—the domination some have always dreamed of. But it is the story of King Midas writ large—the power looks nothing like what we thought it would. It is a brutish, cloddish power, not a creative one. We sit astride the world like some military dictator, some smelly Papa Doc—we are able to wreak violence with great efficiency and to destroy all that is good and worthwhile, but not to exercise power to any real end. And, ultimately, that violence threatens us. Forget the interplanetary Rose Bowl; "man's synthetic future" has more to do with not going out in the sun for fear of cancer.

BUT THE CANCER and the rising sea level and the other physical effects are still in the future. For now, let's concentrate on what it feels like to live on a planet where nature is no longer nature. What is the sadness about?

In the first place, merely the knowledge that we screwed up. It may have been an inevitable divorce: man, so powerful, may not have been meant to live forever within the constraints of nature. It may have been an inevitable progression—man growing up to be stronger than his mother, nature. But even inevitable passages such as these are attended by grief. Ambition, growth take us away from old comforts and assurances. We are used to the idea that something larger than we are and not of our own making surrounds us, that there is a world of man and a world of nature. And we cling to that idea in part because it makes that world of men easier to deal with. E. B. White, in one of his last essays, written from his salt-water farm near Mt. Desert in Maine, said that "with so much disturbing our lives and clouding our future . . . it is hard to foretell what is going to happen." But, he continued, "I know one thing that *has* happened: the willow by the brook has slipped into her yellow dress, lending, along with the faded pink of the snow fence, a spot of color to the vast gray-and-white world. I know, too, that on some not too distant night, somewhere in pond or ditch or low place, a frog will awake, raise his voice in praise, and be joined by others. I will feel a whole lot better when I hear the frogs." There may still be frogs—there may be *more* frogs, for all I know—but they will be messengers not from another world, whose permanence and routine can comfort us, but from a world that is of our own making, as surely as Manhattan is of our own making. And while Manhattan has many virtues, I have never heard anyone say that its sounds make you feel certain that the world, and you in it, are safe.

Anyway, I don't think that this separation was an inevitable divorce, the genetically programmed growth of a child. I think it was a mistake, and that consciously or unconsciously many of us realize it was a mistake, and that this adds to the sadness. Many have fought to keep this day from coming to pass—fought local battles, it is true, perhaps without realizing exactly what was at stake, but still understanding that the independent world of nature was gravely threatened. By the late 1960s an "environmental consciousness" had emerged, and in the 1970s and 1980s real progress was being made: air pollution in many cities had been reduced, and wilderness set aside, and Erie, the dead lake, that symbol of ultimate degradation, rescued from the grave.

So there is the sadness of losing something we've begun to fight for, and the added sadness, or shame, of realizing how much more we could have done—a sadness that shades into self-loathing. We, all of us in the First World, have participated in something of a binge, a half century of unbelievable prosperity and ease. We may have had some intuition that it *was* a binge and the earth couldn't support it, but aside from the easy things (biodegradable detergent, slightly smaller cars) we didn't do much. We didn't turn our lives around to prevent it. Our sadness is almost an aesthetic response— appropriate because we have marred a great, mad, profligate work of art, taken a hammer to the most perfectly proportioned of sculptures.

THERE IS ALSO another emotional response—one that corresponds to the cry "What will I do without him?" when someone vital dies.

I took a day's hike last fall, walking Mill Creek from the spot where it runs by my door to the place where it crosses the main county road near Wevertown. It's a distance of maybe nine miles as the car flies, but rivers are far less efficient, and endlessly follow pointless, time-wasting, uneconomical meanders and curves. Mill Creek cuts some fancy figures, and so I was able to feel a bit exploratory—a budget Bob Marshall. In a strict sense, it wasn't much of an adventure. I stopped at the store for a liverwurst sandwich at lunchtime, the path was generally downhill, the temperature stuck at an equable 55 degrees, and since it was the week before the hunting season opened I didn't have to sing as I walked to keep from getting shot. On the other hand, I had made an arbitrary plan—to follow the creek—and, as a consequence, I spent hours stumbling through overgrown marsh, batting at ten-foot saplings and vines, emerging only every now and then, scratched and weary, into the steeper wooded sections. When Thoreau was on Katahdin, nature said to him, "I have never made this soil for thy feet, this air for thy breathing, these rocks for thy neighbors. I cannot pity nor fondle thee there, but forever relentlessly drive thee hence to where I *am* kind. Why seek me where I have not called thee, and then complain because you find me but a stepmother?" Nature said this to me on Mill Creek, or at least it said, "Go home and tell your wife you walked to Wevertown." I felt I should have carried a machete, or employed a macheteist. (The worst thing about battling through brake and bramble of this sort is that it's so anonymous—gray sticks, green stalks with reddish thorns, none of them to be found in any of the many guides and almanacs on my shelf.) And though I started the day with eight dry socks, none saw noon in that pleasant state.

If it was all a little damp and in a minor key, the sky was nonetheless bright blue, and rabbits kept popping out from my path, and pheasants fired up between my legs, and at each turning some new gift appeared: a vein of quartz, or a ridge where the maples still held their leaves, or a pine more than three feet in diameter that beavers had gnawed all the way around and halfway through and then left standing—a forty-foot sculpture. It was October, so there weren't even any bugs. And always the plash of the stream in my ear. It isn't Yosemite, the Mill Creek Valley, but its small beauties are absorbing, and one can say with Muir on his mountaintop, "Up here all the world's prizes seem as nothing."

And so what if it isn't nature primeval? One of our neighbors has left several kitchen chairs along his stretch of the bank, spaced at fifty-yard intervals for comfort in fishing. At one old homestead, a stone chimney stands at either end of a foundation now filled by a graceful birch. Near the one real waterfall, a lot of rusty pipe and collapsed concrete testifies to the old mill that once stood there. But these aren't disturbing sights—they're almost comforting, reminders of the way that nature has endured and outlived and with dignity reclaimed so many schemes and disruptions of man. (A mile or so off the creek, there's a mine where a hundred and fifty years ago visionary tried to extract pigment for paint and pack it out on mule and sledge. He rebuilt after a fire; finally an avalanche convinced him. The path in is faint now, but his chimney, too, still stands, a small Angkor Wat of free enterprise.) Large sections of the area were once farmed; but the growing season is not more than a hundred days, and the limits established by that higher authority were stronger than the (powerful) attempts of individual men to circumvent them, and so the farms returned to forest, with only a dump of ancient bottles or a section of stone wall as a memorial. (Last fall, though, my wife and I found, in one abandoned meadow, a hop vine planted at least a century before. It was still flowering, and with its blossoms we brewed beer.) These ruins are humbling sights, reminders of the negotiations with nature that have established the world as we know it.

Changing socks (soaking for merely clammy) in front of the waterfall, I thought back to the spring before last, when a record snowfall melted in only a dozen or so warm April days. A little to the south, an inflamed stream washed out a highway bridge, closing the New York Thruway for months. Mill Creek filled till it was a river, and this waterfall, normally one of those diaphanous-veil affairs, turned into a cataract. It filled me with awe to stand there then, on the shaking ground, and think, This is what nature is capable of.

But as I sat there this time, and thought about the dry summer we'd just come through, there was nothing awe inspiring or instructive, or even lulling, in the fall of the water. It suddenly seemed less like a waterfall than like a spillway to accommodate the overflow of a reservoir. That didn't decrease its beauty, but it changed its meaning. It has begun or will soon begin to rain and snow when the particular mix of chemicals we've injected into the atmosphere adds up to rain or snow—when they make it hot enough over some tropical sea to form a cloud and send it this way. I had no more control, in one sense, over this process than I ever did. But it felt different, and lonelier. Instead of a world where rain had an independent and mysterious existence, the rain had become a subset of human activity: a phenomenon like smog or commerce or the noise from the skidder towing logs on Cleveland Road—all things over which I had no control, either. The rain bore a brand; it was a steer, not a deer. And that was where the loneliness came from. There's nothing there except us. There's no such thing as nature anymore—that other world that isn't business and art and breakfast is now not another world, and there is nothing except us alone.

At the same time that I felt lonely, though, I also felt crowded, without privacy. We go to the woods in part to escape. But now there is nothing except us and so there is no escaping other people. As I walked in the autumn woods I saw a lot of sick trees. With the conifers, I suspected acid rain. (At least I have the luxury of only suspecting; in too many places, they *know*.) And so who walked with me in the woods? Well, there were the presidents of the Midwest utilities who kept explaining why they had to burn coal to make electricity (cheaper, fiduciary responsibility, no *proof* it kills trees) and then there were the congressmen who couldn't bring themselves to do anything about it (personally favor but politics the art of compromise, very busy with the war on drugs) and before long the whole human race had arrived to explain its aspirations. We like to drive, they said, air-conditioning is a necessity nowadays, let's go to the mall. By this point, the woods were pretty densely populated. As I attempted to escape, I slipped on another rock, and in I went again. Of course, the person I was fleeing most fearfully was myself, for I drive (I drove forty thousand miles one year), and I'm burning a collapsed barn behind the house next week because it is much the cheapest way to deal with it, and I live on about four hundred times what Thoreau conclusively proved was enough, so I've done my share to take this independent, eternal world and turn it into a science-fair project (and not even a good science-fair project but a cloddish one, like pumping poison into an ant farm and "observing the effects").

The walk along Mill Creek, or any stream, or up any hill, or through any woods, is changed forever—changed as profoundly as when it shifted from pristine and untracked wilderness to mapped and deeded and cultivated land. Our local shopping mall now has a club of people who go "mall walking" every day. They circle the shopping center en masse—Caldor to Sears to J. C. Penney, circuit after circuit with an occasional break to shop. This seems less absurd to me now than it did at first. I like to walk in the outdoors not solely because the air is cleaner but because outdoors we venture into a sphere larger than ourselves. Mall walking involves too many other people, and too many purely human sights, ever to be more than good-natured exercise. But now, out in the wild, the sunshine on one's shoulders is a reminder that man has cracked the ozone, that, thanks to us, the atmosphere absorbs where once it released.

The greenhouse effect is a more apt name than those who coined it imagined. The carbon dioxide and trace gases act like the panes of glass on a greenhouse—the analogy is accurate. But it's more than that. We have built a greenhouse, *a human creation*, where once there bloomed a sweet and wild garden.

Part II
THE NEAR FUTURE

A Promise Broken

A HURRICANE DRAWS its might from the heat transferred to the atmosphere when ocean water evaporates. The warmer the ocean's surface, and the farther beneath the surface the warm water runs, the more powerful the hurricane. If the sea turns cold a few meters beneath the top, the winds of the hurricane will soon churn up that frigid water and the storm will brake itself. But if the warm water runs deep—and in the tropics it may stretch down a hundred and fifty meters or more—the hurricane can build and build. Under present conditions—tropical ocean temperatures of about 80 degrees Fahrenheit—Hurricane Gilbert, which formed off the Windward Islands in the autumn of 1988, approached what Massachusetts Institute of Technology professor Kerry Emanuel has calculated as the upper bound of intensity for a hurricane. The atmospheric pressure at its center dropped to about 885 millibars, and so its winds reached two hundred miles per hour. It can't get any worse than that—under present conditions.

But we switch now from the present to the future. Say the global temperature increased, and as one result the temperature of the ocean went up. A rise of 3 or 4 degrees Fahrenheit in tropical sea-surface temperatures would cause the upper limit of hurricane strength to grow. In the middle of these warmer storms, atmospheric pressure could fall to 800 millibars; as a result, the destructive potential of these superhurricanes would grow between 40 and 50 percent—a Gilbert and a half.

We have killed off nature—that world entirely independent of us which was here before we arrived and which encircled and supported our human society. There's still something out there, though; in the place of the old nature rears up a new "nature" of our own devising. It is like the old nature in that it makes its points through what we think of as natural processes (rain, wind, heat), but it offers none of the consolations—the retreat from the human world, the sense of permanence, and even of eternity. Instead, each cubic yard of air, each square foot of soil, is stamped indelibly with our crude imprint, our X. A lot that has been written about the greenhouse effect has stressed the violence of this retuned nature— the withering heat waves, the drought, the sea rising to flood streets. It certainly makes dramatic sense to imagine this break with nature as one of those messy divorces where the ex-husband turns up drunk and waving a gun. But it may, on the other hand, be a nature of longer growing seasons and fewer harsh winters. We don't know, can't know.

Simply because it bears our mark doesn't mean we can control it. This new "nature" may not be predictably violent. It won't be predictably *anything*, and therefore it will take us a very long time to work out our relationship with it, if ever do. The salient characteristic of this new nature is its unpredictability, just as the salient feature of the old nature was its utter dependability. That may sound strange, for we are used to thinking of the manifestations of nature—rain or sunshine, say—as devious, hard to predict. And over short time spans and for particular places they are; the most cheerful and boisterous weathermen are no more reliable in their forecasts than the cheerful and boisterous sportscasters seated next to them. But on any larger scale nature has been quite constant, and on a global scale it has been a model of reliability. In fact, it has been *the* model of reliability—"as sure as summer follows spring."

Where I live, it is safe to plant tomatoes after June 10, and foolish to plant them before May 20; the last frost is almost sure to fall in those three weeks. In the fall, the first frost nearly always shows up at the beginning of September, and there's a killing freeze by month's end. As a consequence there are no farms nearby. There were once—people tried to grow crops on the land for a generation or so after the initial settlement, but the farms failed, people gave up, and now you come across neat stone walls five miles through the forest from any road. And it's the same in other places; virtually all settlement patterns testify to the dependability of nature. Every year during the late summer, the Nile overflows its banks (or did until the Aswan Dam was built). A pilot knows how the air will behave along his flight path—that a tropical air mass in summer over the American Southeast will breed thunderstorms. ("The details," one meteorologist has said, "are as multifarious as geography itself, but much of it has by now been put into manuals.")

Even extreme events, weather emergencies, have been fairly predictable. Mary Austin, in one of her fine essays on the American desert, wrote that storms "have habits to be learned, appointed paths, seasons, and warnings, and they leave you in no doubt about their performances. One who builds his house on a water scar or the rubble of a steep slope must take his chances." Engineers calculate every drainage and wall for the ability to withstand the "hundred-year storm." Every developer who builds a resort along the coast, every underwriter who insures a ship or a plane, does so with a conscious dependence on the reliability of nature. And even more dependent are those of us who rely *unconsciously* on nature's past performance. The farmer, it is true, has always watched for rain, and sometimes his crops have shriveled. But those of us who do our harvesting at the Price Chopper never doubt that enough rain will fall on enough farms, and it always has.

It is this very predictability that has allowed most of us in the Western world to forget about nature, or to assign it a new role—as a place for withdrawing from the cares of the human world. In some parts of the world, nature has been more capricious, withholding the rain one year or two, pouring it down by the lakeful the next. In these places people think about the weather, about nature, more than we do. But even in Bangladesh people have known that for the most part nature would support them—not richly, but support them.

In this unconscious assumption we mimic animals and plants; as

Loren Eiseley says, the "inorganic world could and does really exist in a kind of chaos, but before life can pop forth, even as a flower, or a stick insect, or a beetle, it has to have some kind of unofficial assurance of nature's stability, just as we read that stability in the ripple marks impressed in stone, or the rain-marks on a long-vanished beach, or the eye of a hundred-million-year-old trilobite." Nineteenth-century biologists, he writes, were "amazed" when they discovered these fossils, "but wasps and migratory birds were not. They had an old contract, an old promise . . . that nature, in degree, is steadfast and continuous." And this promise has enabled life to establish itself even in the places we think of as harsh, since they have been harsh in a fairly dependable way. Mary Austin, for instance, writes of the water trails of the desert—paths that lead to the old and trusty springs. "The crested quail that troop in the Ceriso are the happiest frequenters of these paths," she writes. "Great floods pour down the trail with that peculiar melting motion of moving quail, twittering, shoving, and shouldering. They splatter into the shallows, drink daintily, shake out small showers over their perfect coats, and melt away into the scrub, preening and pranking, with soft contented noises." There is change, says Eiseley, but it is change at "the slow pace of inorganic life," and the seasons never "come and go too violently." This is "nature's promise—a guarantee that has not been broken in four billion years that the universe has a queer kind of rationality and expectedness about it."

That promise was long since broken for passenger pigeons, and for the salmon who ran into dams on the ancestral streams, and for peregrine falcons who found their eggshells so weakened by DDT that they couldn't reproduce. But now it is broken for us, too—nature's lifetime warranty has expired.

The measure of change has gone from the millennium to the decade; we are altering the climate, says Stephen Schneider of the National Center for Atmospheric Research, at a rate ten to sixty times its natural rate of change. The long-range climate forecasts for particular cities made by some researchers are, he says, "somewhat meaningless," and the actual outcome of a general heating could be far different—"better," "worse," but mainly just *different*—from our educated guesses. "Unfortunately," says Schneider, "there is no time over Earth's history that we can turn to when the carbon dioxide amounts in the atmosphere were, say, twice what they are now, and at the same time examine instruments that tell us what the earth's climate was then. . . . Instead we must base our estimates on natural analogs of large climatic change and climatic models." One analog is the Arctic, which biologists, for climatological reasons, have long characterized as "stressed," or "accident-prone," less able to absorb disaster than the milder temperate and tropic zones. Barry Lopez offers an example of this in his *Arctic Dreams:* "In the fall of 1973 an October rainstorm created a layer of ground ice that, later, muskoxen could not break through to feed. Nearly 75 percent of the muskox population in the Canadian archipelago perished that winter." Our climate is not likely ever to be as harsh as the weather currently found above the Arctic Circle, but it is not likely to be as forgiving as the "natural" weather we are used to.

IT MAY TURN OUT that we're not much more suited by our genes to quick adaptation than the musk ox. "Large animals charging, rocks falling, children crying, fires starting—these are the sort of short-range changes that our ancestors had to react to," the population specialist Paul Ehrlich has written. "But the world of 276,824 B.C. was much like that of 276,804 B.C." Still, even if our knack for adaptation proves hardy—and, after all, boat people moving from Cambodia to Canada go through much more severe climatic shifts than anything the scientists forecast—the stress will be continuous, unrelenting, because no one knows how all this will turn out. "The only thing objectively good about the current atmosphere and climate is that they are the ones we are used to," David Doniger of the Natural Resources Defense Council said a few years ago. "Life and civilization are adapted to this environment: change necessarily will be disruptive." It will likely be worst, of course, for those already living on the edge, already subject to nature's whim—out on the floodplains of Bangladesh. But it will affect, at the very least, the mind of each of us. We are not necessarily doomed to suffer some cataclysm. But we can't count on not being so doomed. Professor Emanuel points out that there is no certainty that an increase in global warmth will push up tropical ocean temperatures and thus hurricane strength; neither is there any certainty that it won't.

The uncertainty itself is the first cataclysm, and perhaps the most profound one. If we can't count on enough snow falling to fill the reservoirs that feed our faucets, or if we have to worry that too much of that water will evaporate in the heat, then the weather report is suddenly going to be leading off the Dan Rather newscast. This tension has already begun to show in some places. In the summer of 1988 New York City burned beneath a terrific heat wave, but no relief was to be found in the nearby oceans where medical waste bobbed in the waves. Instead of the usual beach reports—water temperature, available space in the parking lot—the papers ran regular dispatches like this one from mid-July: "The beaches on the southeastern shore of Staten Island, including South and Midland beaches, which have been closed since Wednesday, remained closed yesterday, and officials said they would stay closed until the tides are free of syringes. No blood vials were found yesterday. . . . In New Jersey, Monmouth County health officials lifted a five-day-old ban on swimming at most of Asbury Park's beaches, but left the ban in force for Ocean Grove. Water quality tests showed that fecal coliform bacteria levels were down, but contaminated water was moving south toward Ocean Grove." Even for people who had no intention of swimming off Staten Island, there was something claustrophobic about those reports; even people who moved by air-conditioned cab from air-conditioned apartment to air-conditioned office tower found themselves thinking about the heat. By summer's end, *Time* (no alarmist rag) was reporting that "on top of the usual chafing at day after day of hot, humid, and hazy" weather, Americans were suffering a "communal attack of the worries." This "fretful mood," in which the "soggy unremitting heat sometimes seemed a symptom of general ecological collapse," the magazine's editors dubbed "ecophobia." People, they said, were asking, "Had the great breakdown begun?"

THE FRETFULNESS can only grow, for it is the natural world that has always provided our chief images of stability, our necessary antidotes to the "fast-paced," "dynamic" human society. Art is no longer eternal, if it ever was; it moves with fruitfly speed from one impulse to another. The tools we use each day are not familiar (I am writing this on a "third-generation" computer, now hopelessly outdated), nor are the foods we eat (once upon a time two eggs over was a "healthy breakfast"). We move physically (I was born in California and grew up on the other edge of the continent) and we move mentally (I was born in the Industrial Era and now live in the Information Age). Even our relationships to other people change—I was born before the sexual revolution and came of age in its wake. Such incredible freedom and creativity is stressful. We want our freedom, in the words of the Cape Cod essayist Robert Finch, "as children want it and need it—within safe bounds." Nature has always provided the "deep, constant rhythms," even if, in our turbocharged and jet-propelled arrogance, we have come to think that we are independent of the earth's basic pulses. We still rely on the earth's "basic integrity and equanimity" to give us a "safe and stable context," Finch says, and, in particular, we rely on the seasons. "The recurring cycles of the year are not simply entertaining phenomena, to be noted at our convenience and for our enjoyment, but signs that the cosmos is still intact, that we remain in something larger and more reliable than our own short-lived enthusiasms. It is for this that we need to know the insects will hibernate, that turtles and warblers will migrate and return, that the tide will retreat, the ice let go, the earth tilt back toward the sun, and the grass reawaken." Despite the dozens of new ways to look at the world—the genetic, the microscopic, the chemical—we are still very much the same people who built Stonehenge so that each year we could make sure the sun really did begin its retreat, the same people who trembled at eclipses. As I write this, it is early December. Yesterday, finally, we had our first real snowfall of the winter, and I could feel myself relaxing a little. I took a hike this afternoon, and the woods that had yesterday seemed too brown for the temperature now seemed right, and the squeak of the dry snow matched the cold, astringent air in my nostrils.

Around our small town, which is stuck out on the edge of a wilderness, people talk about the weather constantly—as people do,

I assume, in every part of the world. This is not because people can't think of anything else to say. It's because the weather *is* important, physically and psychologically. Unless there's a storm, the conversations are less about the weather that day than about the signs for the future. ("Did you get frost up your place last night? Time to start splitting wood.") It is the oldest way of saying that deep down all is right with the world. It may have been an arrogant comfort ("What are we / The beast that walks upright with speaking lips / And little hair, to think we should always be fed, / sheltered, intact, and self-controlled?" asked Robinson Jeffers), but it was how we saw the earth. Edwin Way Teale, a twentieth-century American naturalist, devoted two decades to four large volumes chronicling spring, summer, fall, and winter across America. (The final volume alone, *Wandering Through Winter*, journeys from south of San Diego on the Mexican line, where the whales pass in their winter migration, to north of Caribou, on Maine's border with Canada, where "we glimpsed one farmhouse in the moonlight buried to its eaves.") He writes, "This we learned from our experience with the four seasons. We want them all. *We want the rounded year.*" And for more, much more, than variety—we want it for reassurance that the wheel still turns, so that we can worry about our human affairs secure in our knowledge of the eternal inhuman.

And it's not merely the annual cycles of renewal that cheer and assure us but also the longer and more dramatic cycles. Thoreau wrote, "I love to see that Nature is so rife with life that myriads can afford to be sacrificed and suffered to prey on one another, that tender organizations can be so serenely squashed out of existence like pulp—tadpoles which herons gobble up, and tortoises and toads run over in the road. . . . With the liability to accident, we must see how little account is to be made of it. . . . Poison is not poisonous after all, nor are any wounds fatal."

Some of our culture's greatest images of reassurance come from religious sources—from the preacher in Ecclesiastes, for instance, who reminds us that for everything there is a season. In his words we discover the apparent meaninglessness and vanity of human life, since, for all our struggle, nothing ever really changes in the universe: "The wind blows to the south and goes round to the north;

round and round goes the wind, and on its circuits the wind returns." But if this dependable cycle is boring it is also comforting: "What has been is what will be, and what has been done is what will be done, and there is nothing new under the sun." A more positive statement of this truth comes from the Sermon on the Mount. "Therefore I tell you," Jesus declares, "do not be anxious about your life, what you shall eat or what you shall drink, nor about your body, what you shall put on. Is not life more than food, and the body more than clothing? Look at the birds of the air: they neither sow nor reap nor gather into barns, and yet your Heavenly Father feeds them. . . . And why are you anxious about clothing?" The certainty of nature—that God's creation or Darwin's or whoever's will provide for us, bountifully, as it always has—is what frees us to be fully human, to be more than simply gatherers of food.

But what will happen—this summer or next summer or some summer soon—as that certainty falters? The birds of the air, returning each winter to South America, find less and less of the forest that is their home; as a result (and as a result of other human changes), there are fewer birds around us each year. Songbirds are a cause for exclamation now, and the spring grows more quiet than before. And we, I think, grow more nervous.

What happens as that certainty falters? "Adventure," said Bob Marshall on the return from his Arctic jaunts, "is wonderful, but there is no doubt that one of its joys is its end. . . . Lying in bed, with no rising rivers, no straying horses, no morrow's route to worry about, we enjoyed a delightful peacefulness." What happens is that adventure ceases to be a joy and becomes a source of fear, for the end of the adventure is not so certain.

What happens as that certainty falters? What happens, I think, is that for those of us who on Sundays say the Lord's Prayer, the vestigial and anachronistic phrase "Give us this day our daily bread," which has in this nation been either a quaint reminder of an earlier time or a symbolic statement, acquires earthy new meaning, a panicky edge. (And that panicky edge is perhaps a little sharper because once upon a time most people lived near enough to nature to have some feeling they could cope with it. At the turn of the century, two-thirds of the American people lived in places with populations of five thousand or less, and most, I imagine, had some land and some idea or another about how to grow their daily bread—information that has not been passed along to most of us in the Information Age.)

But the first thing that happens as that certainty falters, I think, is the replacement of one idea of the world with another. Instead of thinking of birds, for instance, as serene, independent, carefree, flitty creatures, we may soon develop a store of pictures like the remarkable one recorded by Mary Austin in *The Land of Little Rain*, her tribute to the California desert published in 1903. Usually, she notes, April, May, and early June are the blossoming, humming months in the desert, after the winter and before the long heat, but once in a while even benign, natural nature misfires, and the heat arrives too early: "The quick increase of suns at the end of spring sometimes overtakes birds in their nesting and effects a reversal of the ordinary manner of incubation. . . . One hot, stifling spring in the Little Antelope I had occasion to pass and repass frequently the nest of a pair of meadowlarks, located unhappily in the shelter of a very slender weed. I never caught them sitting except near night, but at midday they stood, or drooped above it, half fainting with pitifully parted bills, between their treasure and the sun." Sometimes, she went on to say, both mother and father stood there together, their wings spread to keep that precious shade on the egg. It is a fitting image for the age we are heading into—for an age when *The New York Times* had above the fold on its front page one day last autumn stories about the Yellowstone fire, the threat to our homes from radon gas, and the rampage of Hurricane Gilbert. Mary Austin, by the way, eventually rigged up a piece of canvas to cast a shadow across the nest. But it is not clear what, if anything, will come to our aid.

THE SCALE OF THIS uncertainty is so enormous that there are even those who see the greenhouse atmosphere yielding an Ice Age. This theory, formulated by John Hamaker, a retired Midwest engineer, and fervently advanced by a number of California disciples, is dismissed by most professional atmospheric scientists, but it gives an interesting sense of the fragility of present arrangements.

Basically, Hamaker and his followers believe that the cycle of ice ages experienced by the planet in recent geologic times has been driven by changes in the concentration of carbon dioxide, which, in turn, are driven by the "mineralization" and "demineralization" of the soil. Over thousands of years the soil is stripped of its minerals—plants remove them as they grow, they leach out, and so on. When this reaches some critical point, the plant life begins to die out, and this causes, for reasons we've already discussed, a massive increase of carbon dioxide in the atmosphere. Then, as the greenhouse effect heats the equator, it causes large amounts of evaporation from tropical waters. The earth's natural climatic currents push the water-laden clouds north, where they cool and lose their moisture as snow—so much snow that eventually some of it remains over the summer, and the huge glaciers of the next Ice Age form. The glaciers, as they move through the higher latitudes, grind the mountains to dust and "remineralize" the soil, at which point plants are once again able to prosper and the cycle begins again.

Now, it is true that the warm periods between ice ages have lasted for fairly regular ten-thousand-year intervals for a long time, and since the present warm period began about ten thousand years ago, there is reason to think we're about due. Though we haven't given it a thought, our climatic future has always been uncertain. But Hamaker and his following argue that the burst of carbon dioxide released by the Industrial Revolution has jump-started the change—in fact, Hamaker says, the worst effects of this new glaciation will become apparent between now and 1995. The worsening winters "we can stand for some time into the future," he writes. "What we cannot stand is for the winters to carry over into the summers and to destroy crops and trees with frosts and freezes." He says it is already too late "to prevent the deaths of hundreds of millions of people from famine," but "there may still be time to prevent the extermination of civilization for another ninety thousand years of glaciation." He recommends, besides an immediate end to the use of fossil fuels and a total halt to the burning of the rain forests, a crash program of "remineralization"—putting every available airplane into service to drop billions of pounds of crushed rock dust on the earth's forests to spur their growth.

Though there is some scientific backing for the idea that ice ages can begin with startling speed (the National Academy of Sciences said in the 1970s that a period of glaciation could be underway within a century), almost all scientific attention has been focused in recent years on the warming. Hamaker dismisses this focus as a mistake and a cover-up. The government, he writes, would rather deal with a problem fifty years away than with one that will happen before the turn of the century. This I doubt—the scientists I talked to were hopelessly sincere. Anyway, most climatologists now attribute ice ages to the so-called Milankovitch cycles, when the earth's wobble, its tilt, and the shape of its orbit varies its dose of solar radiation. "I'm not saying there's no chance they're right," says Stephen Schneider of the Ice Age theorists, "but it's down below the first decimal point of probability."

That it's even a possibility, however, testifies to our poor understanding of the system we've knocked out of kilter, and to its immense power. Some people will undoubtedly find comfort in such uncertainty, just as some people still rely on those scientists in the pay of the tobacco companies who insist that there is no "proof" of the link between cigarettes and cancer. But it is a superficial comfort, a whistling in the heat. Uncertainty is often seen as nicer than grim certainty, because we, being human, tend to imagine that the happiest outcomes are likely. Maybe we don't need to do anything! For more than a decade, no one did anything about acid rain because some scientists said that our understanding was incomplete, that we didn't know all the chemical interactions and so we had better study some more before spending the sums necessary to clean the obvious sources of pollution. The increase in carbon dioxide has evoked, and will evoke, the same kind of reactions. But, powerful though the uncertainties are—and terrifying, too—they are uncertainties about horrors. How bad will the hurricanes get? Fire or ice? These are not comforting uncertainties—not the lady or the tiger. This is the lion or the tiger.

The uncertainties we are used to dealing with—political uncertainties, such as "Is the budget deficit a real problem?" and personal uncertainties, such as "Should I take this job?"—do not unduly alarm us only because they occur amid general political and personal stability. We live, in the Western world, amid abundance. Most of us have pensions and retirement accounts and certificates of deposit and plans for the future, all of them based on the world operating pretty much as it has always operated. It is in that context that our uncertainties occur. The world around us reassures us: if we don't take this job or marry this woman, we will get another chance. But what happens when that context itself is a source of fear? When the world around us is going crazy? It will be a little like living in wartime, I think, when only the most basic reassurances— the belief, say, that one will go to heaven when one dies—will matter.

MOST OF THE EFFECTS that scientists are starting to predict stem from the heating of the earth, the 3- to 8-degree rise in average global temperature that is the consensus prediction for the near future. It doesn't require great imagination to see that this will change our lives, but it takes powerful computers to give a hint of just how. And even the powerful computers often disagree. The three main American models of a global warming (Hansen's NASA projections, a program devised at Oregon State University, and another at the National Oceanic and Atmospheric Administration) predict widely different results for the continental United States. The NASA model predicts increased summer precipitation in the Great Lakes region, for instance, while the NOAA program yields a decrease, and Oregon's figures it won't change at all. In the meantime, though, there are plenty of scenarios.

The single most-talked-about consequence is probably the expected rise in global sea level as a result of polar melting. For the last few thousand years, the sea level "has risen so slowly that for most practical purposes it has been constant," says James Titus, of the Environmental Protection Agency. As a result, people have developed the coastlines extensively. Not just the beaches in Rio or the canals in Venice, but also the infrastructure of all major ports, around which have grown up most of the world's great cities. And not just people: marine plants and animals have taken the opportunity provided by sea-level stability to build huge communities such as the one in Chesapeake Bay. But, despite all this confidence, the sea level is not a given. A hundred thousand years ago, during the last interglacial period, it was twenty feet above the current levels; at the height of the last Ice Age, when much of the world's water was frozen at the poles, the sea level fell three hundred feet. Scientists estimate that the world's remaining ice cover contains enough water so that if it should all melt the sea level would rise about 75 meters, or nearly 250 feet. This potential inundation is stored in the Greenland Ice Sheet (if it melts it will raise the world's oceans twenty feet), the West Antarctic Ice Sheet (another twenty feet), and East Antarctica (nearly two hundred feet), with a smaller amount, perhaps one and a half feet, in all the planet's alpine glaciers combined. (Melting the ice currently over water, such as the sea ice of the Arctic Ocean, won't raise the sea level, any more than a melting ice cube overflows a gin and tonic.) As the East Antarctic is considered safe, the direst fears of a rising sea came as the result of a 1968 study that concluded that the Ross and Filchner-Ronne ice shelves supporting the West Antarctic Ice Sheet could disintegrate within forty years, swelling the oceans seven meters, or twenty-three feet. Subsequent investigations, however, seem to have demonstrated that such a disintegration would take at least two centuries, and probably more like five (though several investigators have speculated that such a deglaciation might become irreversible within the next century).

However, the salvation of the West Antarctic does not mean the salvation of Bangladesh, or even of East Hampton. A number of other factors seem ready to raise the sea level significantly. The alpine glaciers, while small compared with the ice caps, are not small. Glaciers bordering the Gulf of Alaska, for instance, have been melting for decades, and constitute a source of fresh water about the size of the entire Mississippi River system. And even if nothing melted at all, the increased heat alone would raise the sea level considerably. Warm water takes up more space than cold water—this thermal expansion, given a global temperature increase of 1.5 to 4.5 degrees Celsius, should raise sea levels a foot, according to Hansen. Two Canadian researchers announced in May 1989 that, according to their measurements of more than four hundred sites, sea level is already rising an inch a decade—it is by now widely accepted that sea level will rise significantly over the next decades. The EPA has estimated that it will increase 144 to 217 centimeters (4.7 to more than seven feet) by 2100, and speculated about worst-case scenarios that might lead to an eleven-foot-plus rise; the National Academy of Sciences has been more conservative, but other researchers have turned in even scarier numbers. Suffice it to say that the best guess of almost every panel and every individual scientist studying the problem includes within its range an increase in global sea level of better than one meter, or 3.3 feet.

That does not sound like so much, but it means that the sea would reach a height unprecedented in the history of civilization. The immediate effects of this swollen sea would be seen in a place like the Maldive Islands. By most accounts, this archipelago of 1,190 small islands about four hundred miles southwest of Sri Lanka sounds fairly paradisaical. Its 187,000 residents had never heard a gun fired in anger until a short-lived coup attempt mounted by foreign mercenaries in 1988. They survived the downturn in the coir business (coir is an elastic fiber made from coconut husks); breadfruit, citron, and fig trees are abundant. The worst criminals are banished to uninhabited outer islands. But most of this happy nation rises only two meters above the Indian Ocean. If the sea level were to rise one meter, storm surges would become an enormous, crippling danger; were it to rise two meters, a rise well within the range of possibilities predicted by many studies, the country would simply disappear. In October 1987 Maldive's president Maumoon Abdul Gayoom went before the United Nations General Assembly. He described his country as "an endangered nation." The Maldivians, he pointed out, "did not contribute to the impending catastrophe . . . and alone we cannot save ourselves." A map drawn in a century may not show the Maldives, except as a danger to mariners.

Other nations, though not extinguished, would be horribly hurt. A two-meter rise in the sea level would flood 20 percent of the land in Bangladesh, much of which is built on the floodplains at the mouth of the Brahmaputra. In Egypt, such a rise would inundate only about 1 percent of the land, but that 1 percent includes much of the Nile delta, where most of the population live. All across Asia, farmers grow rice on low river deltas and floodplains. Because those farmers lack the resources to build dikes and seawalls (and in some places, such as Bangladesh, such defenses are practically impossible), harvests would almost certainly fall.

But it is not just the Third World. A couple of years ago, the United States Environmental Protection Agency issued a worksheet whereby local governments could calculate their future position vis-à-vis the salt water. (In Sandy Hook, New Jersey, for instance, add thirteen inches to account for local geologic subsidence to the projected increases in sea level, for a net ocean rise of four feet one inch.) Direct inundation of land would cause a certain number of problems; in Massachusetts, for instance, between three thousand and ten thousand acres of oceanfront land worth between $3 billion and $10 billion might disappear by 2025, and that figure does not include land lost to growing ponds and bogs as the rising sea lifts the water table. But storm surges would do the most dramatic damage. In Galveston, Texas, 98 percent of the land is within the plain that would be flooded by the worst storms. Such surges are the reason that Holland built its protective dikes. The most extensive barriers went up after the winter of 1953, when a surge breached the existing dikes in eighty-nine places along the central delta, killing nearly two thousand people and tens of thousands of cattle. Afterward the Dutch decided to spend more than $3 billion building new defenses.

As the Dutch effort indicates, much can be done to defend against increases in the sea level. The literature abounds with studies on how much it would cost to protect coastal areas. Researchers, for instance, have worked out three methods to save Long Beach Island, an eight-mile-long barrier island off the New Jersey coast: it could be encircled with a levee, or gradually raised by adding sand, or allowed to "migrate" landward by piling new sand on its inland edge as sand was eroded from the front. The levee would be the cheapest solution at only about $800 million, but the money would have to be spent all at once. ("Moreover," commented one of the researchers, "a levee would eliminate the waterfront view.") Allowing the island to migrate landward, on the other hand, would cost a staggering $7.7 *billion*, mainly because all the roads and utilities would have to be repeatedly ripped up and moved. So, with interest rates and the like figured in, the cheapest method would be to gradually raise the island by gradually adding sand—a bargain at $1,706,000,000.

The exactness of such figures provides a sense of comfort, but almost certainly a false one. Though each study is filled with footnotes on topics like "the sensitivity of sand costs to increasing scarcity," the estimated cost of doing anything on a very large scale—even something like building a missile, which can be done under controlled conditions—is invariably off. Any numbers are at best a guess, useful only as a way of saying "big problem, very big problem." The estimates of the cost of protecting the sheltered shoreline of America alone run as high as $80 billion; add barrier islands and so on and the cost of defending against a 6-foot rise in sea level might top $300 billion according to the experts. In Holland, nearly six cents of every dollar of the gross national product is already spent on holding back the sea.

Still, it's only money, and it would probably be worth it to save our beaches, especially since the warmer greenhouse weather would increase the need for a day at the shore. (A study, of course, has quantified this relationship. Ocean City, Maryland, it found, might hold back a one-foot sea-level rise by spending about twenty-five cents per visitor, which would be well within its means, because the warm weather might increase its total tourist revenues 25 percent.) The trouble is, spending the money to protect the shoreline would lead to ecological costs harder to enumerate but easy to understand.

Coastal marshes or wetlands exist in a nearly unbroken chain along the Gulf and Atlantic coasts of the United States. Part land and part water, they are more "biologically productive" than either the ocean or the dry land. The tide flows in and out, spreading food and flushing out waste—a cycle that encourages quick growth and rapid decay. Protected from the waves of the ocean by barrier islands or sand dunes or peninsulas, these peaceful communities are used by an immense variety of birds, fish, shellfish, and plants. "All organic life is beautifully and variedly adjusted to the conditions of its environment," wrote biologist James Morris, "but it is doubtful if in any other zone of the organic world the accommodations are more exquisitely ordered than in the marshes of the ocean shore." This fact was not always appreciated; early settlers, with noble exceptions such as Bartram, thought these coastal marshes "miasmal" and drained or filled many of them. In recent years, though, federal and state authorities have grudgingly begun to protect them. In the fall of 1988, a panel of "governors, businessmen, and environmentalists" chaired by New Jersey governor Thomas Kean compared the continuing loss of wetlands to development to "the Texas chainsaw massacre" and proposed that the government in the future allow "no net loss" of the remaining wetlands. As King Canute demonstrated, however, the ocean disregards governments, and, presumably, even blue-ribbon commissions, and as its level rises the area of the wetlands will dwindle. This is not axiomatic: if the marsh has room and time enough to back up slowly, it will, and the drowned wetland will be replaced by a new one. But as a government report pointed out last July, "in most areas, the slope above the marsh is steeper than the marsh; so a rise in sea level causes a net loss of marsh acreage"—that is, in many cases the marsh will run into a cliff it can't climb.

In some places—along the coast of Maine, say—the cliffs are natural. But in many other places they may be man made, like the levee proposed for Long Beach Island. If I have a house on Cape Cod, and my choice is to build a wall in front of it or to let a marsh come in and colonize my basement, I will likely build the wall. (There are a lot of houses like this. As Joseph Siry notes in a recent book about wetlands, the growth of the American population since the Depression has centered only generally on the states of the Sunbelt; more specifically, it has been along the coasts of those states.) What this wall building will mean if the sea level rises is truly staggering. Should the ocean go up a meter, at least half the nation's coastal wetlands could be lost. But, said the EPA, "most of today's wetland shorelines still would have wetlands; the strip would simply be narrower. By contrast, protecting all mainland areas would generally mean replacing natural shorelines with bulkheads and levees. "This distinction," the relentlessly practical authors add, "is important because for many species of fish, the length of a wetland shoreline is more critical than the total area." It is also important if you are used to the idea of the ocean meeting the land with ease and grace, not bumping into an endless cement wall.

THERE ARE OTHER REASONS, too, to fear a sea-level rise. A few years ago I spent a happy day with William Harkness, the rivermaster of the Delaware River. He has an office in Milford, Pennsylvania, and a little tower a few miles away on the river, right at a prime shad-fishing bend. Essentially, his job is to watch the Delaware to see how much water flows past each day. If the flow drops below a certain level, he orders the City of New York, which maintains several great reservoirs on the upper reaches of the river, to release water downstream instead of piping it east to the city. The rivermaster's job results from several decades of litigation between New York City and the communities, especially Philadelphia, near the mouth of the Delaware. Under the agreement, New York must release enough water to keep the "salt front"—the ocean—from advancing up the river. In normal times the water pouring out of a river pushes the ocean back, but in a drought the reduced flow creates a vacuum, which the sea oozes in to fill. During the drought of the 1960s, said Harkness, the salt front nearly reached Philadelphia's water intakes. "It didn't, but that's something you worry about," he said. "Everyone in Philly turning on a tap and getting salt water."

The only problem with the present arrangement is that during a drought, when New York must release vast quantities of water down the Delaware to hold the salt front back, New Yorkers continue to take showers and wash their hands. During the last severe northeastern drought, in the summer of 1985, city officials made up for the diminished flow from the Delaware by pumping water straight from the Hudson. This worked well—the water turned out to be considerably cleaner than many had feared—but as the flow of the Hudson was reduced the salt front began to creep up *that* river, and the town fathers of Poughkeepsie became very worried about *their* supply getting salty. As the greenhouse warming kicks in, increased evaporation could steal 10 to 24 percent of the water in New York's reservoirs, the EPA concluded; in addition, a one-meter sea-level rise could push the salt front up past the city's water intakes on the Hudson. In all, says the government, "doubled carbon dioxide could produce a shortfall equal to twenty-eight to forty-two percent of planned supply in the Hudson River Basin." Which, in turn, worries me, because the city's water engineers have always looked covetously at the Adirondacks as a possible source of supply, even though they are more than two hundred miles distant. When the Catskill reservoirs were built early in this century, they drowned several small towns and miles of wild land; the same thing will happen if they build a set of reservoirs here. As I have been saying, complications pile upon complications—and pretty soon my vegetable garden is under forty feet of drinking water.

THE EXPECTED EFFECTS of a sea-level rise typify the many consequences of a global warming. On the one hand, they are so big we literally can't understand them. If there is a significant polar melting, the earth's center of gravity will shift, tipping the globe in such a way that the sea level might actually drop at Cape Horn and along the coast of Iceland—I read this in a recent EPA report and found that I didn't really understand what it meant to tip the earth, though I was awed by the idea. On the other hand, the changes ultimately acquire a quite personal dimension: Should I put in a wall in front of my house? Does this taste salty to you? And, most telling of all, the human response to the problems, the utterly natural human attempt to preserve the old natural way of life in this postnatural world, creates entirely new consequences. The ocean rises; I build a wall; the marsh dies, and, with it, the fish.

What's more, many of the various effects of the warming compound one another. If the weather grows hotter and I take more showers, more water must be diverted from the river, and the salt front moves upstream, and so on. The contradictions multiply almost endlessly (more air-conditioning means more power gener-

ated means more water sucked from the rivers to cool the genera-
tors means less water flowing downstream, et cetera ad infinitum).
These aren't the simple complications of, say, the summer of 1988,
when the hot weather drove everyone on the East Coast to the
beaches, only to discover the tide of syringes. These contradictions
are the result of throwing every single system into an uproar at the
same time, so that none of nature's reliable compensations can be
counted on.

For example, at the same time that the sea level is increasing and
the warmer air can gather up more water vapor, and, presumably,
the overall precipitation will be increasing, the temperature is also
going up. The result, say the computer modelers, will be greatly increased levels of evaporation, and, in many parts of the world, a
drier interior to match the sodden coasts.

It's not simply a matter of heat. If the temperature rises, the
number of days with snow cover will likely fall. When the snow-
melting season ends, more of the sun's energy is absorbed by the
ground instead of being reflected back to space and as a result the
soil begins to dry out. In the greenhouse world, however, this pattern of seasonal change happens earlier because the snow melts
sooner. Along with such increases go changes in the weather, of
course. In some parts of the world these may offset some of the
evaporation—Roger Revelle, the Scripps climatologist, once estimated that flows along the Niger, the Senegal, the Volta, the Blue
Nile, the Mekong, and the Brahmaputra would increase, probably
with disastrous results in the latter two cases, while flows might diminish in the Hwang Ho in China, and the Amu Darya and Syr
Darya (which run through Russia's principal agricultural areas), the
Tigris-Euphrates, and the Zambezi. The United States, as usual,
has been most closely studied. America is blessed with ample
water—on an average day 4,200 billion gallons of rain fall on the
lower forty-eight states. Most of that evaporates, leaving only about
1,435 billion gallons a day, of which, in 1985, only about 340 billion
gallons a day are withdrawn for human use. It seems like more than
enough. However, as anyone who has ever flown across the nation
(and looked out the window) can attest, the water is not spread
evenly. Vast sections of the West are arid, though not necessarily

unpopulated. Total water use exceeds average stream flow in twenty-four of fifty-three western water-resource regions, a difference made up by "mining" dwindling groundwater stocks and importing water. Much of the Colorado's flow, for example, is dammed, diverted, and consumed upstream by irrigation and by the millions upon millions of people living (and insisting on green lawns) where it would otherwise be too dry.

And matters may get much worse. After studying the temperature and stream flow records, scientists have concluded that if a "conservative" 2-degree Celsius increase in temperature occurs, the virgin flow of the Colorado could fall by nearly a third. If, as some of the computer models suggest, this is accompanied by a 10 percent fall in precipitation in the Southwest as the result of new weather patterns, water supply in the upper Colorado could fall by 40 percent, but even if precipitation went up 10 percent, runoff would still drop nearly a fifth. Across the West, the picture is similar—in the Missouri, Arkansas, Texas Gulf, and California irrigation regions, runoff could fall by 40 percent or more. In the Missouri, Rio Grande, and Colorado basins, even current water needs could not be met by stream flows after the expected climatic changes. "One model we're looking at," says Texas agriculture commissioner Jim Hightower, "predicts a twenty-five percent increase in the demand for irrigation water" from the Ogallala aquifer, the great subterranean lake that irrigates the plains and is already badly depleted. "You can't pump more water if the well has already gone dry."

Even areas that we're used to thinking of as ruined may be ruined in new and interesting ways. Lake Erie and the Great Lakes in general became symbols of environmental decline in the 1970s. They have recovered somewhat, but a change in climate may subject them to unprecedented stresses (which is like subjecting the South Bronx to unprecedented decay). Under EPA models of doubled carbon dioxide levels the average level of Lake Superior could fall by a foot and a half—which doesn't sound like so much, except that the fleet of ships working the Great Lakes are designed to pass within a foot of the bottom of the locks and channels. Ships will have to carry smaller loads and sail more frequently (burning more fuel, which will—you know). Shippers may be aided by a longer shipping season. The central basin of Lake Erie currently sees eighty-three days of ice, but if the temperatures rise, only areas near shore will freeze, and then for three weeks or less. But in that case the erosion along the shoreline, which has been protected by the ice, will increase, since the winter is the season of big storms. And if the ships do keep sailing, it may also increase the supply of sad folk songs—it was a winter gale in 1975 that sank the *Edmund Fitzgerald* with all twenty-nine hands.

Declining water levels can cause a variety of miscellaneous mischief. When droughts lowered Lake Michigan in the 1960s, dry rot set in along the piers and pilings of Chicago's shoreline. Hydropower production may drop as flows along the Niagara River fall, pollutants in the lakes may become less diluted, and the warmer lake waters will almost certainly lead to algal blooms and a return of the oxygen deprivation that "killed" Lake Erie once before. That "increased eutrophication could make the Lake Erie Central Basin uninhabitable for finfish and shellfish during the summer," concluded the EPA.

Across the country and across the world the usual endless list of multiplying dangers can be compiled. "Water quality appears to be vulnerable to deterioration because of increased use of agricultural pesticides as a response to climate change," reported the EPA. There is an increased risk of forest fires like 1988's Yellowstone blaze ("The biggest difference between this year and other years is no rain," the park ecologist Donald Despain said after the fire). As usual, no one knows exactly what will happen. But, the computer model used by Syukuro Manabe, of the National Oceanic and Atmospheric Administration, insists there's a greater than 90 percent chance that soil moisture across North America, western Europe, and Siberia will decrease.

AN OBVIOUS QUESTION is what all this means for agriculture (or, since "agriculture" has become abstracted from everyday life in the same fashion as, say, "the military," it might be better to ask what this will mean as regards dinner). The answer comes on several levels, the first that of the individual plant. Quite apart from heat and drought, the simple increase in the amount of carbon dioxide in the atmosphere affects plants. Ninety percent of the dry weight of a plant comes from the conversion of carbon dioxide to carbohydrates by photosynthesis. If nothing else limits a plant's growth—if it has plenty of sunshine, water, and nutrients—then increased carbon dioxide should increase the yield. And in ideal laboratory conditions this is what happens; as a result, some journalists have rhapsodized about "supercucumbers," and found other green linings to the cloud of greenhouse gases. But there are drawbacks. If some crops grow more quickly, farmers may need to buy more fertilizer. Leaves may become richer in carbon but poorer in nitrogen, reducing food quality not only for humans but for nitrogen-craving insects who may eat more leaf to get their fix. In the best case, direct effects of increased carbon dioxide on yield are expected to be small: annual harvests of well-tended corn crops might rise about 5 percent when carbon dioxide levels reach four hundred parts per million, all other things being equal.

But all other things, of course, won't be equal. All other things—moisture, temperature, growing season—will be different. It is an obvious point, but one worth repeating: everything we eat, except fish and a few hothouse vegetables, spends its growing life in the open air, "exposed," in the words of biologist Paul Waggoner, "to the annual lottery of the weather." Today's Lean Cuisine frozen entrée stood rooted in some Kansas field last year, where it survived attacks from insects and disease, and grew as fast as its supply of water and sunshine and nutrients allowed. About fifty million acres of America's cropland and rangeland is irrigated, but even that depends on the weather over any long stretch. And we can't just stick the wheat crop under glass.

It is a tricky business trying to predict what changes in the weather will do to crops. A longer growing season—the period between frosts—obviously helps; a lack of moisture obviously hurts. If temperatures stay warm, plants grow nicely. If temperatures get really hot, plants wither; a long stretch above 95 degrees Fahrenheit, for instance, means that corn won't fertilize. The climate models are too crude to project with any precision what will happen in a given area, though that fact hasn't stopped scientists from trying. As I write this, I have by my side two thick volumes from the United Nations Environmental Programme about climate change and agriculture. Seventy-six scientists from seventeen nations contributed to the report. Should a drought of the severity of the one in 1936 recur in Saskatchewan, farmers working dark brown soils would spend, provincewide, $28,000 less on lubricating oil. Carcass weight of Icelandic sheep falls 802 grams for every degree Celsius decrease in the mean annual temperature, at least in the Arneshreppur district. Should the temperature warm, Japan would suffer a "very severe rice surplus," especially since most of the rest of the world prefers *indica* rice to *japonica*, limiting the export market. The town of Ouricuri will increase its cowpea yield more than five other towns in northeastern Brazil if precipitation should increase 10 percent and evaporation drop an identical amount. If late-winter absolute temperature minima were to increase by about .8 degree Celsius, thus decreasing the frost risk, the upper limit of cultivation on the slopes of the Ecuadoran sierra might rise two hundred meters to the four-thousand-meter mark.

Similar studies have been done for the United States. The potato leafhopper, a serious pest to soybeans, at present spends the winter in a narrow band along the Gulf of Mexico, but, says the EPA, the warmer temperatures in the computer models "suggest a doubling or tripling of the overwintering range," and thus an increase in "the invasion populations in the northern states by similar factors." Higher winter temperatures "may lower the incidence of respiratory diseases in livestock," but hotter summers will almost certainly "increase the costs of air-conditioning in poultry housing." The horn fly already causes annual losses of $730.3 million in the beef and dairy-cattle industries; if warm weather extended its season by eight or ten weeks, milk production could significantly decrease.

The uncertainty ahead, in other words, extends to the pastures and the fields—to our food supply. Too many unknowns and too many variables make even the broadest predictions difficult. Looking back at the severe droughts of the Dust Bowl years provides scant guidance: on the one hand, the technological revolution in agriculture has tripled yields since that time, but, on the other hand, as the EPA noted, "the economic robustness associated with general multiple-enterprise farms has long since passed from the scene on any significant scale," and therefore, "the current vulnerability of our agricultural system to climate change may be greater in some ways than it was in the past."

Consequently, most of the experts have simply thrown up their hands. The guesses seem to be mostly that the northern reaches of the Soviet Union and Canada will be able to grow more food and the Great Plains of the United States less—not so little that America couldn't feed itself but enough below present production that U.S. food exports, which earn the country between $35 billion and $40 billion in a good year, might fall by 70 percent. "It has been suggested," Stephen Schneider, of the National Center for Atmospheric Research, told Congress last summer, "that a future with soil moisture change would translate to a loss of comparative advantage of U.S. agricultural products on the world market"—a phrase to make an economist shiver on an August day.

As USUAL, there is a strong temptation to clutch at every reassurance: if the models say there will be enough food to go around, *whew!* But when computers are modeling something as complex as all of agriculture, the potential for error is enormous (or the potential for accuracy is small). The effect of the heat and drought of 1988 made liars of most of the computer programs in just a few weeks. They had concluded that a doubling of carbon dioxide, which will not happen for several decades, might make the weather hot and dry enough to cut American corn and soybean yields as much as 27 percent. But in the summer of 1988, when the rains held off, the American corn crop fell over 35 percent, down 2.6 *billion* bushels. The summer of 1988 was like the Antarctic ozone hole: it showed up in none of the models.

Even if the heat wave had little to do with the greenhouse effect, we now have some idea of what it will feel like once it does kick in. By early this year, grain storage around the world amounted to only about 250 million metric tons, enough to last fifty-four days—the lowest level since 1973. Worldwide consumption of grain outpaced worldwide production by 152 million metric tons last year. One can run a budget deficit for quite a while, but when the food runs out there's no central bank to mint some more. A second year of drought would be a "catastrophe," the assistant secretary of agriculture said. "If we return to a normal situation in the weather, we'll be okay," said Nelson Denlinger, executive vice president of the United States Wheat Association.

But there is no normal situation in the weather to return to—that's the point. The weather of the future cannot be predicted from the weather of the past, nor can its effects. Paul Waggoner, in a National Academy of Sciences report published in 1983, concluded that "the safest prediction of any we shall make is: farmers will adapt to a change in climate, exploiting it and making our preceding predictions too pessimistic." But farmers depend on the past; that is the source of their skill. All of a sudden, they are like Ethiopian tribesmen hurling spears against Italian tanks. The chance for surprises grows as fast as the changes in the weather. Last fall, when American farmers finally harvested what corn crop there was and took it to the grain elevators, United States Department of Agriculture officials began to find new trouble: corn samples from at least seven states—including Iowa, Illinois, and Indiana, which grow close to half the nation's crop—were found to be contaminated with aflatoxin, a fungus commonly found in topsoil. When overheated corn kernels crack, the mold rushes in. Aflatoxin is a potent carcinogen, known to cause liver cancer, and corn for human consumption can't contain more than twenty parts per billion, while immature hogs are limited to a hundred parts per billion and mature cattle to three hundred. As federal inspectors examined harvests under ultraviolet light, an alarming percentage glowed with the fungus; as much as 70 percent of the fields in northeast Texas had aflatoxin levels above the highest acceptable level, reported *The New York Times*, and forty dairies there had to dump milk from cows fed infected grain. In some cases the corn could be mixed with uncontaminated grain and the aflatoxin levels thus reduced enough to be used as cattle feed; still, an FDA official said, it was a "severe problem." And it had never occurred to me—or, I suspect, to anyone else who wasn't a corn farmer—that it might happen.

The thing to remember, as I have said before, is that all these various changes may be happening at once: it's hotter, and it's drier, and the sea level is rising as fast as food prices, and the horn fly is spreading, and the hurricanes strengthening, and so on. And not the least of it is the simple fact of daily life in a hotter climate. The American summer of 1988, when no one talked about anything but the heat and when it would end, was, on average, only a degree or two warmer than what we were used to. But the models predict summer could soon be 5 or 6 or 7 degrees warmer than the old "normal." Science has yet to devise a way of measuring what percentage of people feel like human beings on any given August afternoon, or counting the number of work hours lost to the third cold bath of the day—or, for that matter, reckoning the lost wit and civility in a population concerned mainly with keeping its shirts dry. These are important matters, and a future full of summers like that is a grim prospect. Summer will come to mean something different—not the carefree season anymore but a time to grit one's teeth and survive. Summer will mean something new in Omaha if the temperature is above 95 degrees fifty days instead of the current thirteen, and in Memphis if it fails to fall below 75 degrees ninety nights a year instead of today's twenty. We can air-condition, of course (though air conditioning pumps carbon into the atmosphere, and air conditioners often require the use of chlorofluorocarbons), and perhaps that will be the new nature's greatest effect. Perhaps summer will become the season when no one goes outdoors. But to anyone who lived through the 1988 heat it seems unlikely we'll simply get used to it.

A certain number of people who didn't get used to that heat died of it. Public health researchers have correlated mortality and temperature tables. When the weather gets hot, they find, preterm births and perinatal deaths both rise. Heart-disease mortality goes up during heat waves and emphysema gets worse. The EPA notes that if "climate change encourages a transition from forest to grassland in some areas, grass pollens could increase," worsening hay fever and asthma. If the number of days between 60 and 95 degrees increases, so will the mosquito population. To the EPA this means that malaria, encephalitis, and dengue fever ("severe pain in the joints," often fatal) might break out in the continental United States, and that there is at least a slight risk of yellow fever and Rift Valley Fever. I find it hard to imagine malaria, but all too easy to conceive of new clouds of mosquitoes harassing me while I weed the garden, or droning by my ear at night. Mosquitoes are bad enough as a force of nature; if we have to blame ourselves for their presence, they may become an unbearable symbol of our folly—our many follies, for it was the desire to be rid of them altogether that led us to poison the world with DDT, of course, and now we may inadvertently enlarge their number.

"A variety of other U.S. diseases indicate a sensitivity to changes in weather," the EPA reports. "Higher humidity may increase the incidence and severity of fungal skin diseases (such as ringworm and athlete's foot) and yeast infections (candidiasis). Studies on soldiers stationed in Vietnam during the war indicated that outpatient visits for skin diseases (the largest single cause of outpatient visits) were directly correlated to increases in humidity." The interesting thing about this last sentence, from the EPA's official report to Congress on the effects of climate change, is less the fact than its source—that a useful place to look for information about the new American weather is Vietnam. There is nothing wrong with the Vietnamese climate—it is not "better" or "worse" than the various American climates, or the weather in Britain, or the cold of Canada. And people have been able to move back and forth between all these zones, adapting to conditions. In fact, we've all often wanted to; a change of climate is perhaps the single biggest inducement to travel. But now the climate is traveling. According to a United Nations study, "the climate of Finland is estimated to become similar to that of northern Germany, of southern Saskatchewan to northern Nebraska, of the Leningrad region to the western Ukraine, of the central Urals to central Norway, of Hokkaido to northern Honshu, and of Iceland to northeast Scotland." If we felt like keeping the weather we're accustomed to, it's we who would have to move, traveling north ahead of the heat.

THE TEMPTATION to spend much time in the sun, reduced by the growing heat, will be further reduced by the erosion of the ozone layer, the health effects of which could be potentially greater than anything stemming from the change in the climate. Ultraviolet radiation is not uniformly dangerous. Ultraviolet A, with wavelengths above 320 nanometers, is necessary for the formation of vitamin D. But the energy in a UV-B photon is much higher than in UV-A; as a result, it can damage cells. In the sunlight we grew up with, ozone and oxygen in the stratosphere screened out much—not all—of the solar radiation with wavelengths between 290 and 320 nanometers. Even at present levels, the UV-B that reaches the earth's surface ages the skin and can cause skin cancer. Since most of the ultraviolet is absorbed in the first few layers of cells, a creature the size of, say, a human being will feel the effects principally on exposed organs—the skin and the eye. It is the melanin pigment in the upper layer that absorbs most of the radiation; however, depending on the amount of melanin, radiation can penetrate to lower levels, exposing basal cells and squamous cells and causing the mutations in them that lead to cancer. One thing this means is that white people are seven to ten times more likely to contract malignant melanoma than blacks. Interestingly, according to studies quoted by the Environmental Policy Institute, this is a disease less of the field hand than of the office worker; it most often affects parts of the body not usually exposed to the sun (the torso, for instance), and seems to come from sunbathing on vacation. A 3 percent decrease in ozone, which is near what scientists have currently observed, would likely produce two hundred thousand additional cases of skin cancer, mostly in North America, Europe, the Soviet Union, Australia, New Zealand, and Japan.

Ultraviolet radiation can also easily damage the human eye. Eskimos have always worn slitted glasses, because snow reflects 80 to 90 percent of the UV-B that strikes it, while vegetation reflects very little; as a result of the snow glare, eyes often swell shut. (Sand reflects 40 percent, so vacationing in Aruba instead of Aspen may not help much.) Photokeratosis, the scientific name for what is more commonly known as snow blindness, is like a sunburn of the eye. It usually heals without permanent injury. But long-term ultraviolet exposure can result in cataracts and then blindness. Cataracts are already a serious problem in the United States. But here, at least, surgeons are available. The 3 percent decrease in ozone, according to the Environmental Policy Institute, would lead to approximately four hundred thousand new cataract cases a year. Many would go blind, especially in the Third World, where people work outside and where a surgeon is a rare thing. Again, as usual, there are a thousand tiny interactions. We have already seen that hot weather increases the number of premature births. And retinal damage leading to blindness in premature babies is believed by many to be connected with ultraviolet radiation. On a larger scale, the ability of farmers to cope with the changes in the weather may be limited if they have to worry about staying out of the sun. If the damage to the ozone turns out to be more severe than is now expected (and so far all the models have been too conservative), some analysts talk about cattle that could only graze at dusk for fear of eye damage, and farmers that might measure their exposure to the sun in minutes—like workers at a nuclear plant.

The increased ultraviolet radiation could also have direct effects on plants, exacerbating many of the problems caused by the warming. At least two hundred plant species have been tested at elevated levels of ultraviolet, and about two-thirds have shown some degree of sensitivity. The increased ultraviolet seems to limit leaf size, cutting the amount of energy the plants could capture from the sun. Peas, beans, squash, melons, and cabbage were found to be especially affected; one study of soybeans (the world's fifth-largest crop) showed that a severe depletion of the ozone could cut yields by a quarter to a half. Ozone loss poses an even greater threat to the small marine animals (zooplankton) and marine plant life (phytoplankton). They are sensitive to ultraviolet because they are so tiny; our skin can absorb most or all of the increased radiation, but it penetrates right to the heart of these organisms. There are indications that many plankton species have already reached their maximum tolerance for ultraviolet radiation. "They are under very drastic ultraviolet stress right now," Donat Haber, of the University of Marburg, in West Germany, told The New York Times last March. "Most of them are incredibly sensitive. When you expose a population of these organisms [to increased levels] they will die within a few hours." In the case of zooplankton, those that do not die may sink lower in the water to avoid the increased ultraviolet, and this cuts the amount of sunlight they receive. A number of zooplankton, including shrimp, apparently tailor their breeding season to make sure they're not on the surface in the summer, when ultraviolet levels are at their height; a 7.5 percent reduction of ozone might cut the shrimp breeding period in half.

Some scientists—notably James Lovelock—think that ozone was not necessary for life's emergence, and argue that certain algae could survive a full dose of ultraviolet. Unfortunately, other studies show that the kinds of plankton that can cope with excess ultraviolet are not as nutritious as the kinds that die. All this is important because the little zooplankton grow into crabs and anchovies and the like, and the little phytoplankton get eaten by larger fish (and some whale species). About half the world's protein comes from marine species, and in Third World countries the percentage is especially high. And—oh, yes—phytoplankton play a key part in the carbon cycle, sucking in vast amounts of carbon dioxide. If a large part of the world's algae die, the greenhouse effect will speed up.

THE LIST of miscellaneous effects that will result from changes in the atmosphere is, literally, infinite: everything down to the proverbial (the price of tea in China, the water in the kitchen sink) changes when the world changes on this scale. Researchers have calculated, for instance, that paint will fade, transparent window glazings yellow, and polymer automobile roofs become "chalky" much more quickly if the ozone layer deteriorates. Ultraviolet radiation damages polyvinyl chloride, requiring that it be manufactured with more titanium oxide, a light stabilizer. By 2075, this could add $4.7 billion to the cost of siding and other PVC products. In New York City the 1988 summer heat increased the effects of leaks from underground steam pipes, softening asphalt and causing thousands of "hummocks," potholes in reverse, in the streets. "When it's over ninety degrees for a prolonged period, it becomes a minor disaster," said Lucius Ricco, of the New York City Bureau of Highway Operations. Steel expansion joints bubbled along Interstate 66 around Washington, D.C., during the heat wave, and a hundred and sixty people were injured when a train derailed in Montana, apparently after the heat warped the rails.

Coupled with the physical predictions are endless political and financial conjectures. If the higher northern latitudes warm 8 degrees or more in winter, as some models project, "the fabled Northwest passage would be open," according to one researcher. "You could sail from Tokyo to Europe in half the time." Politics could change; Francis Bretherton, of the National Center for Atmospheric Research, told *Time* that if the Great Plains became a dust bowl and people followed the seasonable temperatures north, Canada might rival the Soviet Union as the world's most powerful nation.

This game can go on forever, swinging from the absurdly specific to the madly speculative. There is no easy way to say that something can't happen or is unlikely to happen; such forecasts are based on the past, and now there is no relevant past. In this case, gauging the future from the past is like predicting that a man can jump the same distance on the moon as on the earth. This uncertainty has very tangible effects: if engineers don't know where the sea level will be, or how much water will flow down a river, they don't know how much concrete to pour. A group of scientists meeting in Austria in 1985 concluded, "Many important economic and social decisions are being made today on major irrigation, hydropower, and other water projects; on drought and agricultural land use, on structural designs and coastal engineering projects; and on energy planning, all based on assumptions about climate a number of decades into the future. Most such decisions assume that past climatic data, without modification, are a reliable guide to the future. This is no longer a good assumption." Jesse Ausubel, director of programs at the National Academy of Engineering, said it may become difficult "to find a site for a dam or an airport or a public transportation system or anything designed to last thirty to forty years. What do you do when the past is no longer a guide to the future?" The problem is, there are no good substitutes—even the men who make the general climate models admit that their projections are crude at the global level, wildly uncertain at any lower one. We are left with a vast collection of "mights," and only one certainty: we have changed the world, and therefore some of the "mights" are inevitable.

OF COURSE, there has always been change, and the future has always been a collection of possibilities. But we have speeded up that change so much that it is really a difference in kind, not quantity. The typical projections of global warming over the next century—an increase of between 2 and 6 degrees Celsius in average temperature—amount to saying that the world's climate will be changing at ten to sixty times its natural speed, Stephen Schneider, of the National Center for Atmospheric Research, has explained. "Ten times is the best possible case," he said in a recent interview. But even ten times is an almost unimaginable acceleration; it's as if we were driving down a highway at sixty miles an hour and suddenly the accelerator got stuck and the brake didn't work and we were doing six hundred miles an hour. The sixty times as fast hardly matters—it probably wouldn't be much more impossible to drive the car at 3,600 miles an hour. The difference would come earlier than that. I've driven a car a hundred miles an hour, maybe a little faster; on the autobahn I guess some cars hit 120, and Jackie Stewart can cruise at two hundred. But past that would be not faster, just different. You couldn't turn or brake or even really see what was whipping past you. Your ability to handle a car at sixty does not prove *anything* about your ability to handle a car at six hundred miles an hour. A car can't be handled at six hundred miles an hour except on the Bonneville Salt Flats. Similarly, our ability to survive the dust bowl years—our ability to survive the heat in the summer of 1988, though with a lowered water table, depleted grain reserves, and so on—is no proof of our ability to survive what's coming.

Even the possible scenarios of future change—the melting ice caps, say—reassure us a little bit, because they let us at least begin to imagine living in that world. We can plan where we might move, and contemplate possible changes in our property values, and whether or not our jobs will still exist. But such reassurance is illusory. "Quite simply, the faster the climate is forced to change, the more likely there will be unexpected surprises lurking," Schneider told Congress.

WHILE AMERICA SWELTERED last summer, scientists on the staff of the Environmental Protection Agency were finishing up the most comprehensive assessment yet made of the possible effects of the climate change. Congress had requested the study two years earlier, and the EPA did its work diligently, studying four regions in great detail and pulling together most of the available literature on the subject. Though the report's authors were not timid in their conclusions, they did insert several caveats. "We have no experience with the rapid warming projected to occur over the next century. We cannot simulate in a laboratory what will happen over the entire North American continent," they wrote. And, they added with ominous modesty, "*The results are also inherently limited by our imaginations. Until a severe event occurs such as the drought of 1988, we fail to recognize the close links between our society, the environment, and climate. For example, in this report we did not analyze or anticipate the reductions in barge shipments due to lower river levels, the increases in forest fires due to dry conditions, or the impacts on ducks due to disappearing prairie potholes.*"

Let's look at that last small item, "the impacts on ducks," for it sums up many of the lessons of this new artificial nature. As everyone knows, the changes already wrought by man have hurt a lot of other species—this has been true since we built the first dam or plowed the first field. And as the changes have accelerated, so has the damage. Only 29 million birds flew up the midcontinental flyways in the spring of 1988, down from a high of 45 million thirty-three years ago when the Fish and Wildlife Service first started counting. But there have also been great efforts in recent years to save enough nature to accommodate at least some ducks (and bears and elk and eagles) and, at least to a certain degree, these efforts have succeeded. In the summer of 1988, however, as ducks flew north they found very little water. Parts of North Dakota were 90 percent dry, and one aerial survey of Canadian prairie, reported

Penny Ward Moser in *Sports Illustrated*, showed only seven of 330 prairie potholes holding water. The potholes were a product of nature's slow pace: when the glaciers retreated ten thousand years ago they left pockmarks on the plains. Over the last hundred years or so, men have drained many of them. And last summer the drought emptied most of the rest. "The strongest of the early arrivals staked a claim, mated, and tried to raise a clutch in rapidly dwindling waters, surrounded by predators who congregated nearby, anticipating a summer-long feast," Moser wrote. Some ducks took one look and decided to forget about mating; they spent the summer floating unproductively on the larger lakes. Others flew farther north, arriving finally at suitable habitat but by then they were too protein-starved to produce eggs. Meanwhile, the ducks that had found potholes to nest in, and had so far survived the lurking predators, began to contract botulism; in the warm and shallow water it became an epidemic. Other ducks—*many* other ducks—died when the United States Department of Agriculture, attempting to aid drought-stricken farmers, released fifty million acres of "set-aside" and conservation land they had been paying the farmers not to touch. As the tractors roared through, they mowed and baled nests and ducks as well as hay. Millions of fish were dying, too, as temperatures soared in streams and lakes, and lowering water levels concentrated pesticides. Moser, on the farm in northern Illinois where she grew up, wrote: "We see no great blue herons in our streams this summer. There are barely any streams at all. The muskrats' underwater tunnels are high in the banks above the water. . . . Hanging over a culvert along the road, we watch some minnows wriggle over mud shallows looking for a deeper pool. Then the minnows reverse direction, pushing over the mud again, back to where they had been. This *is* the deeper pool."

This is not one country's sadness, nor is it the story of a single year. Animals and plants that live in refuges around the world may soon find their "sanctuaries" and "preserves" unendurable traps. If the forests indeed die as the weather warms, many animals will go with them; as the EPA report points out, the fig wasp is at a loss without the fig tree and vice versa. Millions of the tiny animals that constitute the coral reefs may already be dying as warmer water kills their main food source, a species of brown algae.

But even if the trees manage to migrate—if the ecosystem avoids a "crash"—wildlife will be in trouble. Animals don't know they're in refuges, and they aren't as adaptable as people. As the temperature warms, the elk will move north out of Yellowstone, and so will the bison and the grizzly and the dozens of other plants and animals that find safety there. When a bison steps across the park line, he is, of course, fair game for hunters, who already line the boundaries at the proper season. The hunting laws can be changed, of course, but hunters are not the only danger the animals face. The way north is cut with roads and fences, crossed by cars, divided up into small chunks. Montana isn't exactly crowded, but a couple of hundred miles (that is, a couple of degrees Celsius) north of Yellowstone Lake you're in Great Falls, which is no place for a bison herd. In the Kalahari desert of Botswana, when a drought sent a quarter million wildebeest north in search of water, incalculable numbers of them died along a hundred-mile fence set up to protect cattle. We have confined nature to small parcels; the shifting climate "will find thousands of species blocked by farm fences and fields, four-lane highways, housing developments, and other man-made barriers as they try to escape to cool safety," Robert L. Peters, of the World Wildlife Fund, writes. "There is reason to believe that the impact on the natural world would rival that of the last Ice Age."

I find myself thinking often of the birds in Mary Austin's desert, or the purple martin chicks near Moser's Illinois farm that "cooked to death" in last summer's heat. They are actual events and also metaphors. The heat will cook the eggs of birds, and that destruction—and the hurricanes and the rising sea and the literally blinding sun—will rob us of our sense of security. There will be no reason to feel secure because there will be no reason to be secure. The old planet is a different planet. That the temperature had never reached 100 degrees at the airport in Glens Falls, the city nearest my home, made it a decent bet that it never would. And then, last summer, it did. There is no good reason anymore to say it won't reach 110 degrees. We live in a different world; therefore, life feels different.

The Defiant Reflex

LAST SUMMER I paddled across a northern Adirondack lake with a state biologist to visit an eagle's nest. Thirty years before, in an effort to curb blackflies, communities in this area put big blocks of DDT in the streams. The blackflies survived (they hung in clouds around us all this morning, contemptuous of pine-scent Old Woodsman), but the eagles, among others, didn't. The chemical thinned the shells of their eggs; when the mother eagles sat on their eggs as they always had, the shells collapsed.

Finally, last year, three pairs of eagles returned to the Adirondacks and built nests. The DDT levels in the water had dropped low enough to allow them back. We sat in the canoe and watched a big eagle circle above us: he was the very eagle from the dollar bill, eyes beady with patient irritation, head ruffled. His mate was on the nest, and we were too close. He swooped nearby; we backed off; he rose with a beat or two of his wings—he had a six-foot wingspan— and flew for the nest. When he got there, he stuck out his wings, stalled, and dropped softly down.

This grand sight I owe to Rachel Carson; had she not written when she did about the dangers of DDT, it might well have been too late before anyone cared about what was happening. She pointed out the problem; she offered a solution; the world shifted course.

That is how this book should end, too. At this writing, the green-house effect shows every sign of emerging as an important political issue—perhaps *the* important political issue. President Bush has scheduled a global scientific workshop on the topic for the fall of 1989; there is much talk of an international convention to draw up a treaty on climate change modeled on the accords to phase out chlorofluorocarbon production. It all sounds promising, rational. There *should* be a solution, and we should write our congressmen about it, and they should enact it, and then we should all get on with our lives. We should come up with a good practical response, a plan, a series of steps, a seven-point proposal to solve the greenhouse effect. That is the modern way. That is our reflex.

But there are reasons—economic and demographic reasons but also reasons of chemistry and physics—to think such an approach won't work so easily in this case, that a "solution" may be difficult, verging on impossible.

The minute, for instance, that the scientists at the 1988 congressional hearings finished explaining that we were heating up the earth, senators began to shout about nuclear power; it was quite literally their first reaction. Senator Wendell Ford of Kentucky, addressing the scientists, said, "Well, half this group, I bet you, a few years ago was against plutonium. . . . And now we have come a hundred and eighty degrees." Asked Senator Frank Murkowski of Alaska, "Is it indeed a reality that we must look more aggressively to nuclear as a release, because I don't see the public demanding any reduction in the power requirements that our air-conditioners run off, everything else that we enjoy." This is the voice of the practical man. Not even the senator from Alaska can imagine life without air-conditioning, and so we *must* come up with some solution, and fast.

But is nuclear power a solution? Lay aside the question of whether it is safe and the question of what we will do with the resulting waste (though it is a sign of the depth of our addiction that we would be willing to lay aside such considerations). Nuclear energy is at the moment and for the foreseeable future useful for generating electricity but not for, say, powering my Honda. To address even the 30 percent of the carbon dioxide created by electric generation (and remember that carbon dioxide is only 50 percent of the total greenhouse gas problem), we would need to build an enormous number of Shorehams and Seabrooks—a process that would take, at the least, decades. Or we would have to wait the "between twenty years and never" one chemist said it would take to even start putting a potential source of electricity like fusion into use. And we have no spare decades: putting off the solution twenty or thirty or forty years gives us another thirty or forty or sixty parts per million carbon dioxide.

Still, what about increasing efficiency? What about conservation? If conservatives instantly think of more reactors, conservation is the liberal reflex. Congress, for instance, is currently considering a bill that would increase gas mileage for cars and light trucks and take a number of other steps—it is known as the "global-warming prevention" bill.

There is—no question about it—waste, even fifteen years after the energy crisis. As just one small example, most of the electricity consumed by industry is used to drive motors. Anticipating expansion, companies tend to buy larger motors than they need; however, large motors are inefficient when they run at less than their optimal speed. If every industrial motor in the United States were to be equipped with available speed-control technology, the latest edition of the *World Resources* yearbook estimates, America's total electricity consumption would fall 7 percent. The typical American water heater, the Natural Resources Defense Council contends, uses 4,500 to 6,000 kilowatt-hours of electricity annually, while state-of-the-art models consume only 800 to 1,200.

We must end such waste, the sooner the better. But are such steps going to *solve* the problem? Consider for a minute a few numbers, supplied by Irving Mintzer, of the World Resources Institute. The numbers are a little dense, but they describe with eloquence the fix we're in. Mintzer outlines a "base case" scenario that "reflects conventional wisdom in its assumptions about technological change, economic growth, and the evolution of the global energy system." In this model, nations do not enact policies to slow carbon-dioxide emissions, or provide more than minimal support for increased energy efficiency and solar research and development, though they do slow the rate of chlorofluorocarbon growth. The result is that by the year 2000 we are committed to an average global warming of 1.6–4.7 degrees Fahrenheit and by 2030 to 2.9–8.5 degrees Fahrenheit. That, says Mintzer, "is by no means the worst possible outcome." If the use of coal and synthetic fuels is encouraged and tropical deforestation continues to increase, then the planet is doomed to a 4.1–12.6 degrees Fahrenheit increase by 2030—numbers with implications too staggering for us to imagine. (By 2075, in this scenario, the globe could be committed to a nearly 30-degree jump. That is even more unimaginable.)

The good news, such as it is, comes in Mintzer's "slow build-up scenario." Under its provisions, strong global efforts to reduce greenhouse-gas emissions "eventually stabilize the atmosphere's composition." Coal, gas, and oil prices are increased sharply, per-capita energy use declines in industrialized countries, and governments dramatically increase support for the development of solar energy. Tropical countries not only cease to cut down the rain forests, but embark on "massive" reforestation efforts. And so on. If all of these heroic efforts had begun in 1980, according to Mintzer's numbers, by 2075 we would be committed to a warming of 2.5–7.5 degrees Fahrenheit. That is still "a warming greater than any experienced in human history." That is to say, if all the liberals and all the conservatives in all the countries of the world had gotten together a decade ago and done all the most dramatic things they could think of, it wouldn't have been enough to prevent terrible, terrible changes.

Why is this? Why can't this problem be solved in the way that, say, DDT was solved? Because, first of all, it's a problem that's different not only in quantity but also in quality. Carbon dioxide and the other greenhouse gases come from *everywhere*, so they can be fixed only by fixing everything. The small substitutions and quick fixes are difficult. Many in Congress, for instance, support the development of methanol-fueled vehicles that emit fewer pollutants like nitrogen oxide. But much methanol would be made with coal—the process could dramatically *increase* levels of carbon dioxide.

The size and complexity of the industrial system we've built makes even the most obvious and immediate changes physically difficult. For instance, one answer that people often suggest for the carbon dioxide crisis is that we plant more trees. And we should—but, as one study showed, enough American sycamores to soak up fifty years of the world's output of carbon dioxide from fossil fuel burning would cover a land area the size of Europe with American sycamore seedlings. And a land area the size of Europe doesn't exist uncovered by crops or desert or ice. Also, say EPA researchers, there may not be enough phosphate, nitrogen, or potash for fertilizer. And acid rain is killing the trees we do have. And as it gets hotter in the next few decades—as a result of carbon dioxide already released—huge tracts of forest may die, as we have seen. And if we plant huge numbers of trees on fallow land, we might change the albedo of the earth. This is a controversial point, but some scientists contend that fewer of the sun's rays would be reflected by the dark green of the trees than the grassland they replace. (One study even estimated that massive tree planting could reduce the earth's reflectivity by 20 percent, increasing the world temperature at a rate roughly equivalent to seven years of carbon-dioxide emissions.) Another common suggestion is to replace much of the coal and oil we burn with natural gas, since it produces only about half as much carbon dioxide. But if natural gas—methane—escapes into the atmosphere *before* it burns, it traps solar radiation twenty times more efficiently than carbon dioxide. And natural gas does leak—from wells, from pipelines, from appliances. Dean Abrahamson, an analyst at the University of Minnesota, says data suggest that 2 to 3 percent of American natural gas escapes unburnt. As a result, switching to natural gas may have no effect on the greenhouse effect. It might even make it worse.

Not only is the industrial system huge, but the trend toward growth is incredibly powerful. At the simplest level, population, the increase continues, if not unabated, just a little abated. In some developing countries 37 percent of the population is under fifteen years of age; in Africa, the figure is 45 percent. Demographers calculate that the world's population may plateau by the middle of the next century. That sounds like good news, but before it happens a population the world already strains to support is expected to double, and perhaps nearly triple. Without a stabilized population, even the most immediate and obvious goals, such as slowing deforestation or cutting fossil fuel use, seem far-fetched. If we double energy efficiency but also double the number of energy users—the math is forbidding.

Over the last century a human life has become a machine for burning petroleum. At least in the West the system that produces excess carbon dioxide is not only huge and growing but also *psychologically* all encompassing. It makes no sense to talk about cars and power plants and so on as if they were something apart from our lives—they *are* our lives. George Orwell, writing before World War II, when this addiction was still in its early stages, said, "The coal miner is a sort of grimy caryatid upon whose shoulders everything that is not grimy is supported. . . . In the metabolism of the western world, the coal miner is second in importance only to the man who ploughs the soil." Now that agriculture depends so heavily on fossil fuels, even that rank is reversed.

In the face of such tidal forces, our traditional answers are like the magic war paint donned by American Indians, which their medicine men assured them would ward off bullets. At best—and at worst—they provide a false sense of security. Take, for instance, the widespread idea that the "free market" will accomplish any necessary goal. The price of oil is currently low and seems set to stay there for a while; when it is below twenty-five dollars per barrel, the economists say, most of the incentive for finding new energy sources disappears. And the easiest—and therefore cheapest—inefficiencies were wrung out of the system during the energy crisis. Governments have already "made what many of them believe are heroic efforts" to cut oil use, concluded a National Academy of Sciences report. Our weird problem is an abundance of resources and a shortage of hard economic reasons not to use them.

But the obvious alternative—international government action—will be almost as difficult. For any program to be a success, we must act not only as individuals and as nations but as a community of nations. "Unless all act together," the Worldwatch Institute warned, "there is little reason to act separately." One trouble, though, is that some countries may perceive themselves as potential "winners" in a climatic change; the Russians, for instance, may decide that the chance of increased harvests from a longer growing season is worth the risk of the global warming. And since the Russians, the Americans, and the Chinese own about 90 percent of the world's coal reserves, any one of them can scuttle progress. The possibilities for other divisions—rich versus poor nations, for instance—are large. Every country has its own forms of despoliation to protect; just as an example, the Canadians, who are forever moaning about their role as the helpless victims of American acid rain, are cutting down the virgin forests of British Columbia at a semi-Brazilian pace. And the fact that decisions must be made now for decades ahead means that, in the words of Deputy Secretary of State for the Environment, Health, and Natural Resources, Richard Benedick, "somehow, political leaders and government processes and budget makers must accustom themselves to a new way of thinking." Of all the quixotic ideas discussed here, that may top the list.

ALL THIS IS not to say we shouldn't act. We must act, and in every way possible, and immediately. We must substitute, conserve, plant trees, perhaps even swallow our concerns over safety and build some nuclear plants. We stand at the end of an era—the hundred years' binge on oil, gas, and coal, which has given us both the comforts and the predicament of the moment. George Woodwell, a Woods Hole marine biologist, who is currently studying the world's forests to discover just how fast they are dying, says we are committed to a warming of several degrees. But if we do not dramatically cut carbon dioxide and other greenhouse gases, the atmosphere will never reach a steady state and "there is virtually no action that can be taken to assure the continuity of natural communities." Even the countries that think they wouldn't mind warming of a degree or two for a longer growing season can't endure an endless heating. There is, Woodwell says, "no question that we've reached the end of the age of fossil fuels." The choice of doing nothing—of continuing to burn ever more oil and coal—is not a choice, in other words. It will lead us, if not straight to hell, then straight to a place with a similar temperature.

There is a small chance that it's too late to avoid such a fate. If conditions change fast enough—if scientists are underestimating the global warming the same way they underestimated the ozone depletion, if we have a sudden greenhouse Ice Age or six straight summers like 1988's—then civilization could rip apart. The futurist Lester Brown has discussed a "domino effect," environmental deterioration leading to rising food prices, producing political unrest. Such conditions would be a perfect culture for the fungus of fanaticism and unreasoning religion. The last time I walked down Fifth Avenue, someone handed me a tract explaining that climate change was a signal of the coming "rapture," and another gave me a pamphlet promising that an understanding of the greenhouse effect could be found in the mysteries of the Kabbalah. Nature has always been the strongest inoculation against this sort of doomsaying. "Familiarity with the ways of the Eternal as they are revealed in the physical universe certainly tends to keep a man sane and sober and safeguards him against the vagaries and half-truths which our creeds and indoor artificial lives tend to breed," wrote John Burroughs. "Think of the obsession of the speedy 'end of the world!' which has so often taken possession of whole communities, as if a world that has been an eternity in forming could end in a day, or on the striking of a clock." When that proof against such obsession begins to crumble, when the earth becomes a model not of permanence but of sudden, unexpected, and devastating change, the number of people seeking an explanation in obscure Scripture or conversations with dead people or a Soviet conspiracy will certainly increase. The chance confluence of this turmoil with the approaching millennium will bring out the low-budget prophets in truly record numbers.

Such a world—a world where people shoot one another in the streets of Boston over a loaf of bread—is not unimaginable. Science fiction writers, survivalists, and gold speculators imagine it all the time. Sometimes I catch myself considering where I might be able to store a year's supply of food, or wondering if I should buy a gun. But if the world is going to deteriorate as rapidly as this, there probably isn't much we can do about it.

What is much more likely is that we will have both the time and the desire to do *something*. The question is: What? A few of the answers are obvious. The destruction of the ozone layer, for instance, can be solved by our ceasing to produce the chemicals currently destroying it. The chlorofluorocarbons and the halons are not essential parts of our industrial base; the Reagan-era Environmental Protection Agency called for a total ban on the chemicals involved, and the European nations have pledged to stop using them by century's end. Though these steps won't end the problem overnight—the chemicals we've already released will reside in the atmosphere for a hundred years or more—they will take care of it eventually. And though the international negotiations may be complex, these steps are easy enough so that they will certainly be taken. The next generation of refrigerators will cost a hundred dollars more—when you get right down to it, big deal. The same with acid rain: Stick scrubbers on the smokestacks. It will cost, but what doesn't? Essentially, it's like controlling DDT, or eating fewer eggs to lower your cholesterol.

But the really big question—the question of global warming—does not yield to the same sort of solution. We can't stop using gasoline the same way we can shut off CFC 12, can't give up heating with oil or cooking with gas as easily as we gave up spraying with DDT. The EPA, in the spring of 1989, proposed a series of "bold actions" for dealing with the greenhouse effect: sharp rises in car mileage, steep drops in home energy use, taxes on fossil fuels. Still, it said, such actions would only slow the buildup of greenhouse gases, not stop them.

With aggressive action, as Mintzer's numbers indicate, we can "stabilize" the situation at some sort of only fairly horrific level, but we cannot resolve it—we can keep the temperature increases at 3 or 4 degrees, not 15 or 30. And Mintzer is not alone in making this sort of calculation. Other forecasters offer even gloomier numbers. The first study on the subject, for instance, done in 1983 by Stephen Seidel and Dale Keyes, of the EPA, concluded that the onset of global warming could not be significantly delayed by changes in policy. Worldwide taxes of as much as 300 percent of the cost of fossil fuels would delay a 2-degree Celsius warming *five years*, from 2040 to 2045, they said; a total ban on coal instituted by the year 2000 would delay it until 2055. "These findings attest to the substantial momentum built into temperature trends," they noted. Therefore, they said, the first implication of their findings was that we should "accelerate and expand research on improving our ability to adapt to a warmer climate." Theirs was an exceedingly pessimistic view, perhaps a little more pessimistic than what more recent measurements support. And we have made progress; the proposed ban on CFCs, for instance, will help significantly with the warming as well as with the ozone loss. Yet even the scientists calling most loudly for controls of emissions say they are doing so in order to slow the *rate* of warming enough that we can adapt. "If the change is slow enough," Stephen Schneider says, "you can study the problems, determine what the regional impacts will be, and learn how to adjust."

THAT ADJUSTMENT—that adaptation—is all that remains to be discussed. There is no question but that we stand near the end of the era of fossil fuels. We have been on a century-long binge, and now the doctor says we must stop drinking—our liver just can't take it anymore.

Were it simply drink, we might well stop; though the addiction to alcohol is powerful, the world is filled with drunks turned sober. But it is not a luxury we are talking about here. It is almost our entire way of life. Our every comfort—the freedom from hard labor, especially, for those of us who enjoy such freedom—depends on this drug. Oil is what has allowed us, finally, to dominate the earth instead of having the earth dominate us. And so we will try to find substitute drugs to give us this same high without further damaging our liver—substitute fuels that won't produce carbon dioxide. But nuclear and solar and so on can't stave off a great heating—that is the meaning of the numbers we've looked at. We've already done too much; there are too many of us; even when we cease to produce carbon dioxide, we still reek of methane.

So we need to "adapt" in some other fashion as well. The question is: How? We could, perhaps, figure out some way to drastically trim our ways of life and our numbers. But our impulse will be to adapt not ourselves but the earth. We will, I think, try to figure out a new way to continue our domination, and hence our accustomed lifestyles, our hopes for our children. This defiance is our reflex. Our impulse will be to spurn the doomsayers and to press bravely ahead into some new world.

After all, while the current *methods* are clearly no longer workable—a few more decades of ungoverned fossil-fuel use and we burn up, to put it bluntly—that does not mean we can't find other ways. To use a loaded analogy, after the crisis of the Civil War slavery was no longer an acceptable method for white Americans to exercise dominion over black Americans. But rather than convert to new notions of universal fellowship and equality white Americans invented segregation, rigging up Jim Crow laws to ensure that much of the old relationship would persist in a new guise. And it is of critical importance to realize that now, just as the old methods of dominating the world have become unworkable, a new set of tools is emerging that may allow us to continue that domination by different, expanded, and even more destructive means—that is, we may very well find a way to keep from choking on our cake, only to gag on the icing later.

The most important of these new tools is genetic engineering, or biotechnology, a staggering development that we will examine in some detail. But we need to understand first that any such new tools are deployed—as the old tools, the oil wells and the chain saws, are deployed—in the service of an ideology, a philosophy. This ideology argues that man is at the center of creation and it is therefore right for him to do whatever pleases him. This notion is deeply ingrained—all of us act on it every day. It is rare to find it plainly argued, but when I was in the library one day I came across a slim volume by a Stanford professor, William F. Baxter, who makes this case explicitly and quite well. He is writing to answer Carson and other environmentalists. "Recently," he says, "scientists have informed us that use of DDT in food production is causing damage to the penguin population. For the present purposes, let us accept that assertion as indisputable scientific fact. The scientific fact is often asserted as if the correct implication—that we must stop agricultural use of DDT—followed from the mere statement of fact about penguin damage. But plainly it does not follow if my criteria are employed."

His criteria include the proposition that "every person should be free to do whatever he wishes in contexts where his actions do not interfere with the interests of other human beings," and that none of our "resources, labors, or skills, should be wasted—that is, employed so as to yield less than they might yield in human satisfaction." The criteria, he says in something of an understatement, "are oriented to people, not penguins. Damage to penguins, or sugar pines, or geological marvels is, without more, simply irrelevant. One must go further, by my criteria, and say: Penguins are important because people enjoy seeing them walk about rocks; and furthermore, the well-being of people would be less impaired by halting use of DDT than by giving up penguins. . . . I have no interest in preserving penguins for their own sake."

It is "undeniably selfish," he admits, "to act as if each person represented one unit of importance and nothing else was of any importance." Nevertheless, he insists, it is the "only tenable" proposition. He lists a number of reasons; other systems, for instance, would not work because no one could represent penguins. ("Penguins cannot vote now and are unlikely subjects for the franchise—pine trees more unlikely still.") While this argument seems silly to me—it does not require any more imagination to figure out which way penguins would vote on DDT than it does to guess how black South Africans would vote on apartheid—his central reason for making man the measure of all is absolutely undeniable. "No other position corresponds to the way most people really think and act—i.e., corresponds to reality." This statement is at the very center of the question. It is an extreme view, but almost all of us, deep down and nitty-gritty, no matter how many environmental petitions we sign, agree with him. That is, we may decide to save the penguins, but if it really were us or them—or even if it were one-twentieth of our comforts or them—the Antarctic would be an empty sheet of ice.

In fact, the few small cracks in this immense structure of belief have come not from moral qualms but from practical fears. When the gas crisis hit, for instance, all of a sudden people began to wonder if maybe our way of life was insupportable. Soon environmentalists were making dire forecasts about everything from aluminum to zinc, and saying we would have to learn to do with less; for a while, it almost became the conventional wisdom.

But a lot of people argued right back in favor of muscular industrialism and the rest of the existing order. The futurist Julian Simon wrote a book, *The Ultimate Resource*, that drove environmentalists crazy with its prediction that before we ran out of anything essential, scientists would figure out new ways to produce it. If we started to run out of copper, he said, we would figure out ways to make it "from other metals." With "knowledge, imagination, and enterprise, we can muster from the earth all the mineral raw materials that we need and desire, at prices that grow smaller relative to other prices and to our total income. In short, our cornucopia is the human mind and heart."

This is not, of course, a scientific argument—he has not figured out the method for producing copper from other metals. It is, despite its reliance on "long-run economic indicators" and such, a religious argument, an article of faith, a perfect example of our defiant impulse. "The main fuel to speed our progress is our stock of knowledge, and the brake is our lack of imagination," Simon writes. "To have more children grow up is also to have more people who can find ways to avert catastrophe."

The essential religiosity (though, since it worships man, it is idolatry) of this view can be easily seen in books like *The Hopeful Future*, where author G. Harry Stine, "one of America's foremost science writers," argues that to forecast using current rates of growth and progress is absurd. Even a curve that assumes that the rate of human progress will continue to increase beyond its current staggering pace is too conservative. Only "Curve E," a "cubic curve, that continues to turn upward ever more steeply with no limit in sight," makes sense. "It means that we can expect eight times as much progress in the next fifty years as we have seen in the last fifty." True, says Stine, this seems "fantastic, impossible, and unbelievable. Things can't possibly happen that way." But "they have in the past, and all indications are they'll continue to do so in the future." This is not, strictly speaking, blind faith, since the optimists can explain their reasoning. But it is *faith*. Believing in something "fantastic, impossible, and unbelievable" is an act of hope as much as of reason. And it comes with other religious trappings—a dark view of people who think differently, for instance. ("Some of the futurists making downside forecasts don't like people. That means they don't like themselves either," chides Stine, in surely the worst put-down possible in the late twentieth century.) And there is a vision of a not too distant utopia. In the twenty-first century, writes Stine, when enormous orbiting satellites beam down "enough energy for everybody to do everything," our main problem will be boredom.

ALMOST ALL OF US intuitively hold this idea of infinite progress, having imbibed it with our infant formula through the sterilized rubber nipple. And quite possibly we are right. We will invent new tools. For example, genetic engineering, which I will examine in greater detail shortly, is an unfathomably powerful technology, at least as powerful as the discovery of fire. It and other new technologies may well allow us to keep our juggling act going, to keep ourselves alive on the planet, to figure out ways to extend our control so completely that nothing, not even the rogue nature we have inadvertently created in our last century of progress, will escape our domination. Perhaps it is too late, and the various feedbacks we may be triggering in the forests and methane sludges will wipe us out. But the defiant optimists like Simon and Stine could as easily be correct in their assertion that we can have a "macromanaged" world—a world where "people and things" are "managed in projects that are very large, very complex, and very lengthy." Such a world might well allow us to continue with our ways of life even in the face of the coming heat. It might be a means of escape. It would replace our brute dominion over the earth with a cleverer, more far-reaching rule.

At the very least, we will almost certainly attempt to create such a future. For it's not only, or even mainly, sybarites who hope we can continue our present domination. (True hedonists rarely think past their next soak in the Jacuzzi.) Mostly it's people with sincere and "progressive" hopes for man. Buckminster Fuller is probably the great example. Fuller was an icon, a guru with a devoted following, and the one time I heard him speak I understood why. Between ten and lunch he covered (in order) the East India Company, Thomas Malthus, royal blood, the discovery of X-rays, electricity as invisible reality, mile-long radio waves, new alloys of metal, the gills of fish, wings of birds, Johannes Kepler, the temporal versus the eternal, the large percentage of the human body that is water, the enormous stresses on ships at sea, why human beings are in the universe, stages in the patent process, eclipses of the moons of Jupiter, DC-4 aircraft, the direction in which a tree falls, and Alexander the Great. Any attempt to summarize the thought of such a man will be crude, but it is fair to say that one thing Fuller believed was that man was not living up to his potential, and that only improvements in technology would allow him to do so.

Fuller was not an enemy of the environment; his geodesic domes, for instance, are as stable as conventional buildings at 3 percent of the weight. Were we all to live in them, there would be a lot more forests standing. But he was first and foremost a champion of man. "We've all been working under the assumption that man is destined to be a failure," he told a crowd twenty years ago. "I say man is quite clearly like the hydrogen atom: designed to be a success. He is a fantastic piece of design." But to be a success man had to advance scientifically. The protesting students of the 1960s, Fuller insisted, operated on the mistaken assumption that the political system needed reforming, when "it is the design science revolution alone that can solve the problem." We have to deal with "our space ship, Earth, as a machine, which is what it is," he said. If engineers increased the overall efficiency of our equipment from 4 percent to 12 percent, Fuller said, "we can take care of all humanity." And so forth. I doubt if he would have viewed the end of nature with much trembling, for he never thought we would or should long stay in the surroundings we had grown accustomed to. Instead, we were like a chick in a shell. The shell had just enough food in it—enough coal and oil and oxygen and whatever—to allow us to develop to a certain point. "But then, by design, the nutriment is exhausted just at the time when the chick is large enough to be able to locomote on its own legs. And so as the chick pecks at the shell seeking more nutriment it inadvertently breaks open the shell." This analogy may be a little selfish. (That there are other species in the shell with us seems not to have crossed his mind.) But it may well be correct, too. We may very well be able to defy the greenhouse effect and press on ahead.

This idea of a managed world has in recent years even acquired the support of a significant group of environmentalist, or at least quasi-environmentalist, thinkers. In the 1970s Dr. James Lovelock, the British scientist who first noted the spread of chlorofluorocarbons through the atmosphere, also formulated what he dubbed the "Gaia hypothesis." This argues that the planet earth is not simply an "environment" for "life" but in fact a living organism, a self-sustaining system, a system that modifies its surroundings so as to ensure its survival. "The atmosphere, the oceans, the climate, and the crust of the earth are regulated at a state comfortable for life *because* of the behavior of living organisms."

This is a stunning argument, first because we are used to thinking of our planet as a chunk of rock covered, by some miracle divine or chemical, with a thin film of life. Instead, say the Gaians, imagine a giant redwood: "The tree is undoubtedly alive, yet ninety-four percent is dead," the inside of the massive trunk a spire of ancient lignin and cellulose surrounded by the current life. But the Gaia hypothesis stuns us for an even larger reason, which is that it seems to imply something is watching over the planet, preserving it. Lovelock takes great pains to show that the planet's self-regulation is automatic, requiring no conscious guidance, no parliament of bacteria. He calls his model of this proof Daisyworld; in its simpler form, it is a computer model of a planet about the same size and the same distance from the sun as the earth but populated only by daisies. Some of the daisies are white, some black, some gray. As with our earth, the sun's heat is growing steadily warmer over billions of years. Daisyworld is without clouds; its temperature, therefore, is determined by the reflectivity of the surface, which in turn depends on the mix of black and white daisies. At first, when the sun is relatively cool, the black daisies grow faster, because they absorb more of the sun's heat. But the spread of dark daisies under those favorable conditions begins to warm the atmosphere, and eventually it grows so hot that the white daisies with their ability to keep cool will have an advantage, and their spread will chill the atmosphere.

This mechanism, of course, requires no more conscious guidance than a furnace hooked to a thermostat. Something very much like this process may have been at work on earth. As the amount of solar energy reaching the earth has increased by more than a quarter over the last three billion years, the amount of heat-trapping carbon dioxide has decreased (until, of course, the frantic human efforts of recent centuries), in the same way that my attic fan turns on when the spring warmth changes to summer heat. Life also created almost all the oxygen in the earth's atmosphere, as we have seen, and for hundreds of millions of years has held its level in the atmosphere at about 21 percent. If it were 15 percent, fires could not begin; were it above 25 percent, even the damp wood of the rain forests would have long since burned in "an awesome conflagration."

The Gaia hypothesis seems, at first blush, to indicate that matters may not be too desperate, that life on the planet will continue regardless of what we do. Lovelock says that this is indeed the case—that the planet will make the necessary adjustments. The earth has dealt with worse problems than the ones we've caused—the rain of planetesimals, for instance, on at least ten occasions inflicted damage that was "comparable in severity to that of a burn affecting sixty percent of the skin of a human," and even a nuclear war would be taken in stride. Those who say that the destruction of the ozone layer would kill almost all life are wrong, according to Lovelock. " 'Earth's fragile shield' is a myth," he writes. "The ozone layer certainly exists today, but it is a flight of fancy to believe that its presence is essential for life."

It is worth bearing in mind, however, that this is "life" he is discussing, not "human life." Gaia, the living organism, is as happy with one-celled wriggling whatevers as she is with mighty man. "Although Gaia may be immune to the eccentricities of some wayward species like us . . . this does not mean that we as a species are also protected from the consequences of our collective folly," he writes.

"Gaia is no doting mother, no fainting damsel. She is a tough virgin, 3.5 billion years old. If a species screws up, she eliminates it with all the feeling of the microbrain in an ICBM." If the world is made unfit by our actions, Gaia will not just find some way to reduce the temperature so we can keep driving Cadillacs; more likely, a new steady state will quickly evolve, and "it is a near certainty that the new state will be less favorable for humans than the one we enjoy now."

Gaian theories should therefore lead, one might think, away from a defiant, human-centered attitude and toward intense respect and solicitousness for the rest of creation. What the world needs, Lovelock has written, is fewer chain saws, cattle, and cars. "It is up to us to act personally in a way that is constructive," he says, and he leads an ecologically sound life on a farm in Cornwall, where he plants trees and rails against "the degraded agricultural monocultures of today with their filthy batteries for cattle and poultry, their ugly-sheet-metal buildings, and roaring, stinking machinery."

Some, however, have misinterpreted the outlines of his idea and implied that it means we need not worry overmuch about pollution or carbon dioxide or whatever—that the world is a giant self-cleaning oven. (They ignore his point that *we* might be the baked-on crud.) A larger group has taken more literally, and more defiantly, his idea of the earth as a living organism, and has decided that if that is the case we must be its brain, that if there is a thermostat we should set it, that we should interfere more and more with the natural processes of the environment.

As a mild example, consider a recent book, *Gaia: An Atlas of Planet Management.* Its editor, Norman Myers, seems absolutely thrilled with the current state of affairs. True, the earth approaches many crises, but they represent "our final evolutionary examination." We must rise to the occasion, pass the test. And we will— "We are grown up. We have acquired the power of life and death for our planet and most of its inhabitants. . . . Our 'satellite vision' means that all the planet's resources—soils, forests, rivers, oceans, minerals—can be not only mapped in fine detail, but vetted for pollution, erosion, or drought; for changes in albedo or humidity; for movements of shoaling fish and migratory creatures." We can process this data at high speed in our computers; we can communicate it around the world instantly. And we can act on it. It is time for man, "as incipient planet managers," to "use this power and use it well." The idea of power is intoxicating, at least to Mr. Myers. "The ancient Greeks, the Renaissance communities, the founders of America, the Victorians enjoyed no such challenge as this," he exults. "What a time to be alive!" If we succeed at the task, the well-known physician Lewis Thomas says in his foreword to the book, "we could become a sort of collective mind for the earth."

This is defiance, continued control, cloaked in a filmy veil of ecological New Age thinking. Most of the actual proposals of these planet managers are sound, the usual suggestions of environmentalists. And in the world we have created they may be necessary, the best we can hope for. But though they love spruce and seed, these "planet managers" have respect mostly for man. They understand that the current methods of domination will overheat the planet, but they have new and improved methods. In their forests of the future, cloned Douglas firs and American sycamores will "sprout like mushrooms," growing straighter, producing "denser wood." Fishermen have always used an inheritance of skill and lore and intuition to figure out where the schools are feeding; but now we can dispense with that romantic inefficiency and replace it with "controlled farming of seaborne wildlife." In fact, almost all wildlife can be kept on ranches, allowing "conservation and profit to go hand in hand."

Even at its most far reaching, though, macromanagement remains a fairly crude method—you may be able to keep track of the fish by satellite, but they're still wild creatures, growing at their own pace. The next step—the step we are about to take—is more sweeping yet.

THE FIRST TIME I really encountered biotechnology, genetic engineering, I was a young reporter covering the weekly meetings of the Cambridge, Massachusetts, City Council. For several years the councillors debated how to regulate the genetic-engineering work then under way at Harvard and MIT. Week after week, Nobel Prize winners and brilliant young researchers would arrive to answer questions; though the liberal councillors from the town's wealthy precincts were skeptical of the scientists, the biggest doubter was Alfred E. Vellucci, the councillor from Italian and Portuguese East Cambridge, who would long ago have won a Nobel himself if only they awarded them for local politics. Gifted with a strong imagination, Vellucci conjured up endless possible scenarios for the accidental release of "these bugs," the reprogrammed organisms scientists were concocting. Could they escape through the sewers? The air-conditioning? On the soles of people's shoes? Eventually, and over the protests of the universities, the city enacted fairly strict regulations governing "containment"—the thickness of doors, and so on. I remember thinking at the time that gene splicing was sort of like nuclear power, potentially useful but risky. It didn't occur to me to think much more deeply about it, to consider ends as well as means.

Nuclear reactors are a new way to create electricity. But genetic engineering is the first way to create new life. It is a staggering idea—"the second big bang," as one biologist put it. It is among the most important scientific advances ever in physical and commercial terms—it is the method that offers the most hope of continuing our way of life, our economic growth, in the teeth of the greenhouse effect. It promises crops that need little water and can survive the heat; it promises cures for the new ailments we are creating as well as the old ones we've yet to solve; it promises survival in almost any environment we may create. It promises total domination.

And for this reason it is without a doubt the most important scientific advance ever in conceptual and moral terms. When I say "moral" I am not thinking primarily of the uses to which such technology might be put—eugenics, say. I am thinking of the very fact of the technology. Jeremy Rifkin, who has emerged as one of the few vigorous opponents of this research (and has covered some of this ground in two fine books, *Algeny* and *Declaration of a Heretic*), says that for thousands of years human beings have lived "pyrotechnically," burning, melting, mixing inanimate materials—coal, say, or iron. We have worked from the outside in to alter our environment. Now we are starting to work from the inside out, and that changes everything. Everything except the driving force, the endless desire to master our planet. As the British writer Brian Stableford declares in his celebratory book, *Future Man*, genetic engineering "will eventually enable us to turn the working of all living things on earth—the entire biosphere—to the particular advantage of our own species." No clearer and crisper definition exists of what I have been calling "defiance."

Watson and Crick described the double helix in 1953. Just twenty years later, in 1973, a pair of American scientists, Stanley Cohen, of Stanford, and Herbert Boyer, of the University of California, took two unrelated organisms—organisms that could not mate in nature, and whose destiny was therefore forever separate—and cut out a piece of DNA from each, then stitched the pieces together. When they were done they had a new form of life, a sort of life that had not existed five minutes before, had not existed until two men got some equipment together and cooked it up.

The next crucial development was the work of the United States Supreme Court, which in 1980 considered the case of Ananda Chakrabarty, a General Electric researcher. Chakrabarty had developed a strain of bacteria that would degrade four of the major components of crude oil; in the event of an oil spill, it could chew up the sludge. In a 5–4 decision, the court held that a man-made microorganism was patentable under current statutes. So not only could man make life; he could make money.

With this spur, research continued to accelerate. In 1981 scientists from Jackson Laboratory, in Bar Harbor, Maine, and the University of Ohio transferred a gene that controlled the manufacture of part of the hemoglobin in rabbits to a mouse embryo, which they brought to term. The mouse was not exactly a mouse; it had a functioning rabbit gene, which it passed on to subsequent generations. This proof of the possibility of animal blends between unrelated species was soon followed by others. English researchers crossed a goat and a sheep, two animals that wouldn't dream of mating in the barnyard (or, if they did, for dreams are widespread, nothing would come of it). A University of Pennsylvania professor managed to insert human growth genes into the fetus of a mouse. When it was born, the mouse grew twice as fast and to twice the size of any other mouse ever. Since it passed the gene on to its offspring, it made forever moot the question "Are you mouse or man?" It was both, and neither.

By the end of 1988, according to a tally in *The New York Times*, there were more than a thousand different strains of such "transgenic" mice, and also twelve breeds of pig, several varieties of rabbits and fish, "at least two breeds of rats and at least one transgenic cow with another still under development." These were mostly experiments; then in the spring of 1988, two Harvard researchers managed to develop another new mouse, this one genetically altered to develop cancer, so that oncologists could use it for studying new treatments. Unlike the earlier inventions, this mouse had commercial possibilities, and was awarded the nation's first animal patent. The patent was licensed to DuPont, and the mice went on sale earlier this year. Fifty dollars apiece. The trade name is Onco-Mouse. Two new brands will be on sale by year's end.

Even those mice, though, will be confined to laboratories (until they escape). A bigger barrier probably fell in April 1987, when Rifkin and other opponents finally ran out of lawsuits, and workers from a company called Advanced Genetic Sciences applied the first genetically engineered bacteria in the great outdoors to a strawberry field in Brentwood, California. Trademarked Frostban, the bacteria employed modified forms of *Pseudomonas syringae* and *Pseudomonas fluorescens;* it was designed to prevent crop losses from frost damage. Some environmental activists ripped up many of the strawberry plants, but it was an empty gesture. A few days later, unmolested, Steven Lindow, the man who had discovered this "ice-nucleating" gene, sprayed Frostban on a field of potato plants in Tule Lake, California.

The pace of this revolution keeps speeding up. Though it has taken more cash than originally expected to bring certain pharmaceuticals to market, over three hundred small companies in the United States alone are trying to invent and market such products; some four hundred genes have been cloned. Several of the ideas I've already mentioned—genetically "improved" trees, for instance—already exist. A Seattle company selects "elite" redwoods from its wild stands, on the basis of such qualities as straightness, height, specific gravity of the wood, and "proper branch drop." Then it clones the trees and plants the wonder seedlings; eventually, the gnarly, crooked trees will be gone from its stands. Classical methods of improving seeds simply do not "adequately satisfy the criteria of the rapid availability of trees of superior quality," one researcher has explained. Christmas-tree growers, threatened by the rise of artificial trees, are now cloning trees with branches that lift upward at the proper 45-degree angle and carry "thick needles that do not fall off to litter the living room floor." A company called Calgene has introduced a gene that gives tobacco plants some resistance to the herbicide glyphosphate (Monsanto's Round-Up to you farmers). The herbicide works by blocking a pathway in plants that synthesizes aromatic amino acids; once the plants have been genetically re-tuned, however, you can spray your fields with the poison without hurting the tobacco. (This example seems significant to me—a way to increase the amount both of the tobacco we can grow and of the chemicals we can spray.) "Genetic engineering of seaweed is just beginning to get under way," declares a Florida researcher. Growth hormone in salmon and trout have been cloned—the trout from Mill Creek, which runs by my door, will doubtless be Arnold Schwarzenegger trout before long.

And this is just the present. The future, the fairly near future, holds so much more, at least in the more fanciful accounts. Brian Stableford, for instance, promises that the "battery chickens" of the future, "whether they are being used to produce eggs or meat," will look very different from the birds of the moment. In fact, the accompanying illustration shows them looking rather like—well, hunks of flesh. This is because, thanks to biotechnology, we might design chickens without the unnecessary heads, wings, and tails. "Nutrients would be pumped in and wastes pumped out through tubes connected to the body." Perhaps we could "grow" lamb chops on an infinite production line, says Stableford, "with red meat and fat attached to an ever-elongating spine of bone." Eventually, all plants might "become unnecessary," replaced by artificial leaves that would "waste" none of the sunlight they receive on luxuries such as roots but instead use "all the energy they trap to make things for us to use."

"Biocosmetics" are not far off, promises Harry Stine—they would permit a "person's physical appearance to be altered to eliminate all unattractive features or marks, and to more closely conform to the currently accepted cultural standards of beauty." And what about night vision, or sonar (although, Stableford says, "this would involve whole new anatomical structures being added to the head," structures that might or might not conform to currently accepted cultural standards of beauty), or double-glazed eyes, for living in space, or the "minor modification" that would allow us to digest cellulose? Headless chickens, tree-eating men—if these are even possible they are far in the future (further in the future, my guess is, than these authors predict). But they are not conceptually different from what we've begun to do in the last twenty years, what we've begun to do in a large way in the last two years—that is, to alter life at its most basic level. The line is not in the distance; the line is here and now, and we have begun to cross, and we shall soon, very soon, be on the other side. If we're not there already.

So THREE CHEERS for us. By dint of our powerful intellects (not my intellect, actually—the intellects of some people at MIT or Oxford or in Japan or wherever) we may have a way out. Just in time—just as the clouds of carbon dioxide threaten to heat the atmosphere and perhaps starve us—we are figuring out a new method of dominating the earth, a method more thorough, and therefore more promising, than burning coal and oil and natural gas. It's not certain that genetic engineering and macromanagement of the world's resources will provide a new cornucopia, but it certainly seems probable. We are a talented species.

Why, then, does it sound so awful? Because, of course, it represents the second end of nature. We have already, pretty much by accident, altered the atmosphere so badly that nature as we know it is over. But this won't be by accident—this will be on purpose. I don't mean that we shall end nature if something goes wrong—if, say, a strain of bacteria programmed to eat cellulose gets loose and eats every tree and weed in sight. And I don't mean we should stop now just so as to prevent the really scary and weird possibilities—the sonar men, the artificial leaves. They are simply novel possible consequences of a more important decision.

It is the simple act of creating new forms of life that changes the world, that puts us forever in the deity business. We will never again be a created being; instead we will be creators. As Rifkin points out, the biotechnologist looks at organisms not as "discrete entities" but as a set of instructions on the computer program that is DNA. It is impossible to have respect for such a set of instructions: they can always be rewritten. And in the view of the researchers they *should* be rewritten, ever improved until they reach some state of absolute efficiency. The only possible measure for such efficiency, of course, is the pleasure of man (and when life can be patented and sold the only real measure of the pleasure of man is the operation of the marketplace). From a chicken's point of view complete efficiency may include a head and feathers and wings; they may very well be integral to what it means to be a chicken. But chickens cannot pay protection money to scientists; if the people, acting through Frank Perdue, decide that it is better to have more efficient—that is, cheaper—chicken, even if it comes from a carcass hooked to a tube, then okay. We will live, eventually, in a shopping mall, where every feature is designed for our delectation.

We have already seen that by pumping carbon dioxide into the air we are artificially lengthening the growing season; in similar fashion, if we spray Frostban on strawberries and artificially lengthen the growing season that way, we have assumed control where once we worked with what we were given. Muir once described the "inexhaustible pages of nature" as "written over and over uncountable times, written in characters of every size and color, sentences composed of sentences, every part of a character a sentence"; not surprisingly, "our limited powers are . . . perplexed and overtaxed" in the attempt to read them. This need no longer be true. Granted, we may never understand the boggling intricacy of the natural world with its niches inside of niches. But we won't need to. The alphabets can all be reduced to mapped strands of DNA. And in this clarity and organization there will be not only efficiency but even a certain beauty, just as there is in a piece of music. Still, perhaps there is more beauty in the cacophony of nature, the "cosmic symphony"? As the British philosopher Leslie Reid once asked, isn't the mind of God incomparably superior even to the mind of Beethoven?

The Gaian atlas I quoted earlier calls for a "new approach to the wild based on rational management rather than on arbitrary exploitation"—that is, herding elk, farming alligators. But after a few years of "rational management" the wild will be the tame. These people are like the public relations officer for an Oregon national forest who kept insisting to me that one reason the Forest Service opposed protecting a prime chunk of land as wilderness was that if it was protected the authorities would then be unable to go in and "improve" the wildlife habitat. "For instance," he said, "you can open up streams where there's a waterfall by blasting the waterfall to create a more gentle grade, so the fish would have a chance to go farther up." I'm not arguing that he's wrong (though, by and large, fish seemed to squeak by before the invention of dynamite). It's just that his concern is for something that looks a lot like nature but isn't.

THERE IS A TENDENCY at every important but difficult crossroad to pretend that it's not really there. We like to imagine that we've already crossed a bridge or not yet come to it. Some people tend not to worry much about genetic engineering, for instance, because they think it's an extension of traditional practices, such as selective breeding. But nature put definite limits on such activity: Mendel could cross two peas, but he couldn't cross a pea with a pine, much less with a pig, much less with a person. We could pen up chickens in atrocious batteries, but they still had heads. There were restraints, in other words—limits. And our understanding of what those limits were helped define nature in our minds. Such notions will quickly become quaint. The idea that nature—that *anything*—could be defined will soon be outdated. Because anything can be changed. A rabbit may be a rabbit for the moment, but tomorrow "rabbit" will have no meaning. "Rabbit" will be a few lines of code, no more important than a set of plans for a 1940 Ford. Why not make rabbit more like dog, or like duck?—whatever suits us. "Our children," Rifkin writes, "will be convinced that their creations are of a far superior nature to those from whom they were copied. . . . They will view all of nature as a computable domain. They will redefine living things as temporal programs that can be edited, revised, and reprogrammed."

In such a world—shifting, without responsibility or moral center, lonely—everything will be possible, eventually including, perhaps, immortality. Why die? What good reason is there? Why age? Why not be kittenish at a hundred and attend the interplanetary Rose Bowl? That must be the reason we have tried so hard to go in this direction. Whether eternal life will have any meaning is another matter. "Eventually," says Stableford, "there may well be a complete breakdown in the distinction between living and non-living—the boundaries between the two will be blurred and filled in by systems which involve both the machinery of life and the machinery of metal, plastic, and glass."

Some of this is speculation, certainly; no one can say with any exactness what will result from a development as awesome as the cracking of the gene. But if that technology falters, some other may emerge. It is the logical outcome of our defiant belief that we must forever dominate the world to our advantage as we have dominated it in the last hundred years. If we are going to go on increasing our numbers, accumulating more possessions, using more resources, then we will have to learn new ways, and genetic engineering and macromanagement seem the most promising.

The problem, in other words, is not simply that burning oil releases carbon dioxide, which happens, by virtue of its molecular structure, to trap the sun's heat. The problem is that nature, the independent force that has surrounded us since our earliest days, cannot coexist with our numbers and our habits. We may well be able to create a world that can support our numbers and our habits, but it will be an artificial world, a space station.

Or, just possibly, we could change our habits.

A Path of More Resistance

SEVERAL YEARS AGO, Jim Stolz shouldered a pack at the Mexican border and hiked eight or nine hundred miles north to the Idaho mountains for a meeting of a small environmental group.

This, he told me as we sat by a stream three months later, was not all that unusual for him. Some years earlier, he had walked the Appalachian Trail, Georgia to Maine. "I spent the next two years going coast to coast. I took the northern route—I spent a couple of months on snowshoes through Wisconsin and Minnesota." He'd never seen the Pacific till he got there on his own two feet. After that, he walked the Continental Divide trail. And then he began to lay out a new trek—the Grand West Trail, he calls it. It runs north and south between the Pacific Crest and the Continental Divide trails, traversing the Grand Canyon and the lava plains, climbing over the Sawtooths. All it lacks is people. "I spent one nine-and-a-half-day stretch this trip when I didn't see anyone," Stolz said. "I see someone else maybe every fourth day."

In the course of his long walks he had twelve times come across grizzly bears, the continent's grandest mammals, now nearly gone from the lower forty-eight. "The last one, he stood on his hind legs, clicked his jaws, woofed three times. I was too close to him, and he was just letting me know. Another one circled me about forty feet away and wouldn't look me in the eye. When you get that close, you realize you're part of the food chain. When we go into grizzly country, we're going into *their* home. We're the intruders. We're used to being top dog. But in griz country we're part of the food chain."

That seemed a quietly radical idea to me—the idea that we don't necessarily belong at the top in every way. It seemed to me, thinking about it later, that it might be a good way to describe a philosophy that is the opposite of the defiant, consumptive course we've traditionally followed. What would it mean to our ways of life, our demographics, our economics, our output of carbon dioxide and methane if we began to truly and viscerally think of ourselves as just one species among many?

The logic of our present thinking—that we should increase in numbers and, especially, in material wealth and ease—leads inexorably in the direction of the managed world. It is, as a few rebels have maintained, a rut, a system of beliefs in which we are trapped. When Thoreau declared that the mass of men lead lives of quiet desperation, it was to this rut that he referred. He went to live at Walden Pond to prove how little man needed to survive—$61.99 $\frac{3}{4}$ for eight months, including the cost of his house.

But most of us have lived in that rut without rebelling. A few, often under Thoreau's influence, may have chucked their sophomore year to live in a tent by some wild lake, but even most of them returned to normal society. Thoreau's explanation—that we think there's no choice—may help explain this fact. But the terrible truth is that most of us rather like the rut. We like acquiring more things; the aphorists notwithstanding, they make us happy. We like the easy life. I was skimming through an old copy of *The New Yorker* not long ago and came across an advertisement, from what in 1949 was still the Esso Company, that summed up our century to this point. "The better you live," it shouted, "the more oil you use." And we live well. The world, as most of us in the West experience it in the late twentieth century, is a reasonably sweet place. That is why there aren't more hippies camped by the lake. We like to camp, but for the weekend.

The only trouble is that this system of beliefs, this pleasant rut, seems not to be making *the planet* happy. The atmosphere and the forests are less satisfied than we are. In fact, they are changing, dying. And those changes affect us, body and soul. The end of nature sours all my material pleasures. The prospect of living in a genetically engineered world sickens me. And yet it is toward such a world that our belief in endless material advancement hurries us.

As long as that desire drives us, there is no way to set limits. We won't develop genetic engineering to eradicate disease and not use it to manufacture perfectly efficient chickens; there is nothing in the logic of our ingrained beliefs that would lead us to draw those lines. Direct our beliefs into a new stream, and that stream will soon be a torrent just like the present one: if we use fusion energy instead of coal, we will still plow ahead at our basic business, accumulation, with all its implications for the natural world. If there is one notion that virtually every successful politician on earth—socialist or fascist or capitalist—agrees on, it is that "economic growth" is good, necessary, the proper end of organized human activity. But where does economic growth end? It ends—or, at least, it runs straight through—the genetically engineered dead world that the optimists envision. That is, provided we can surmount our present environmental troubles.

THOSE TROUBLES, though, just might give us the chance to change the way we think. What if they gave us a practical—as opposed to a moral or an aesthetic—reason to climb out of our rut and find a new one that leads in some different direction? A reason based on atmospheric chemistry, not Eastern spirituality. That is why Stolz's phrase caught my ear, his notion that we might be no more important than anything else. If a new idea—a *humble* idea, in contrast to the conventional defiant attitude—is going to rise out of the wreckage we have made of the world, this is the gut feeling, the impulse, it will come from.

The idea that the rest of creation might count for as much as we do is spectacularly foreign, even to most environmentalists. The ecological movement has always had its greatest success in convincing people that we are threatened by some looming problem—or, if we are not threatened directly, then some creature that we find appealing, such as the seal or the whale or the songbird. The tropical rain forests must be saved because they contain millions of species of plants that may have medical uses—that was the single most common argument against tropical deforestation until it was replaced by the greenhouse effect. Even the American wilderness movement, in some ways a radical crusade, has argued for wilderness largely as places for man—places big enough for backpackers to lose themselves in and for stressed city dwellers to find themselves.

But what if we began to believe in the rain forest *for its own sake?* This attitude has very slowly begun to spread in recent years, both in America and abroad, as the effects of man's domination have become clearer. Some few people have begun to talk of two views of the world—the traditional, man-centered—anthropocentric—view and the biocentric vision of people as a part of the world, just like bears.

Many of those who take the biocentric view are, of course, oddballs, the sort who would walk two thousand miles instead of flying. (Prophets, false or true, are inevitably oddballs. There's not much need for prophets who are in synch with their society.) And theirs is, admittedly, a radical idea, almost an unrealistic idea. It strikes at the root of our identities. But we live at a radical, unrealistic moment. We live at the end of nature, the moment when the essential character of the world we've known since we stopped swinging from our tails is suddenly changing. I'm not intrinsically attracted to radical ideas anymore. I have a house, and a bank account, and I'd like my life, all other things being equal, to continue in its current course. But all other things are not equal—we live at an odd moment in human history when the most basic elements of our lives are changing. I love the trees outside my window; they are a part of my life. I don't want to see them shrivel in the heat, nor sprout in perfect cloned rows. The damage we have done to the planet, and the damage we seem set to do in a genetically engineered business-as-usual future, make me wonder if there isn't some other way. If there isn't a humbler alternative—one that would let us hew closer to what remains of nature, and give it room to recover, if it can. An alternative that would involve changing not only the way we act but also the way we think.

SUCH IDEAS are not brand new. Almost as far back as people have gathered in societies, there are records of ascetics and hermits. Thoreau diluted the religion in this strain of thinking and injected it into the modern bloodstream, but, as we have seen, he went to the woods to redeem man, not nature. (It is curious, in fact, just how little description of nature *Walden* contains.) His is an intensely anthropocentric account—man's desecration of nature worried him less than man's desecration of himself. Nature mattered, but as a wonderful text. "Let us spend one day as deliberately as Nature," he pleads, "and not be thrown off the track by every nutshell and mosquito wing that falls on the rails. Let us rise early and fast, or break fast, gently and without perturbation." Nature was a lesson.

The crucial next step in the development of this humble philosophy—the idea that the rest of creation mattered for its own sake, and that man didn't matter all that much—awaited other writers. It is implicit throughout the works of John Muir, and sometimes it is explicit. In the journal of his thousand-mile hike to the Gulf of Mexico, for instance, there is a passage that stands in perfect contrast to Professor Baxter's argument that men matter entirely and penguins not at all. Muir is writing about alligators, animals as revolting by our standards as any on the continent. He acknowledges that alligators "cannot be called the friends of man" (though he had heard of "one big fellow that was caught young and partially civilized and made to work in harness"). But that, he declares, is not the point. "Many good people believe the alligators were created by the Devil, thus accounting for their all-consuming appetite and ugliness. But doubtless these creatures are happy and fill the place assigned for them by the great Creator of us all. Fierce and cruel they appear to us, but beautiful in the eyes of God." This is more than an ecological, Darwinian vision; it is a moral one: "How narrow we selfish, conceited creatures are in our sympathies! How blind to the rights of all the rest of creation! . . . Though alligators, snakes etc. naturally repel us, they are not mysterious evils. They dwell happily in these flowery wilds, are part of God's family, unfallen, unde-praved, and cared for with the same species of tenderness as is be-stowed on angels in heaven or saints on earth." Muir ends his swampy sermonette with a benediction that stands as a good epi-gram for this humbler approach: "Honorable representatives of the great saurians of older creation, may you long enjoy your lilies and rushes, and be blessed now and then with a mouthful of terror-stricken man by way of dainty!"

Of the many heirs to this philosophical tradition, the most strik-ing was Edward Abbey. A funny, moving novelist and an able critic, Abbey was, more than anything else, an apostle of a place—the desert Southwest, where he lived for many years. Abbey, who died in the spring of 1989, spent long stretches working for the govern-ment in various fire towers and ranger shacks—long stretches ut-terly alone. And alone in the part of nature—the desert—that seems least hospitable, most alienating. Though he loved the desert's beauty, he also recognized its overwhelming alienness. In one of the essays in his first collection he wrote: "The desert says nothing. Completely passive, acted upon but never acting, the desert lies there like the bare skeleton of Being, spare, sparse, austere, utterly worthless, inviting not love but contemplation. In its simplicity and order it suggests the classical, except that *the desert is a realm beyond the human* and in the classicist view only the human is regarded as significant or even recognized as real."

The idea of "a realm beyond the human" but still on this earth is at odds with our deepest notions, our sense of all creation as our private domain. It is no accident that Abbey wrote from the desert. If you lived in the Garden of Eden, or even in, say, Fort Lauderdale, it might be possible to think that the earth had been made for you and your pleasure. But not if you lived in the desert of the South-west. If the desert was made for you, why is there so little water? It's infinitely more plausible that the desert was made for buzzards.

No wonder, then, that in all the world the desert of the South-west was one of the last places left more or less untouched. Prospec-tors had come and gone, and their traces could still be seen in the preserving sand, but when Abbey arrived most of the area lay in its natural state. As a result, he got to watch the developers, miners, and promoters lay their defiant siege to the land. Abbey wrote a novel, *The Monkey Wrench Gang*, out of his anger at the uranium mines and the copper smelters fouling the clean air, and at the endless road building and river damming. Though it is an "action novel," a wild account of a campaign of sabotage against bulldozers and dams, it crystallizes in a single scene the difference between our conventional, defiant view of the world and the biocentric vision.

Early in the book, Hayduke, the hero, decides to disrupt the construction of a road that is being laid out through the Arizona desert. As he follows the planned route, pulling up the surveyor's orange flags, he comes to the stony rim of a small canyon. On the opposite wall, four hundred feet away, he could see the line of stakes, with their Day-Glo ribbons, marching on. "This canyon, then, was going to be bridged. It was only a small and little known canyon, to be sure, with a tiny stream coursing down its bed, meandering in lazy bights over the sand, lolling in pools under the acid-green leafery of the cottonwoods, falling over lip of stone into basin below, barely enough water even in spring to sustain a resident population of spotted toads, red-winged dragonflies, a snake or two, a few canyon wrens, nothing special. And yet Hayduke demurred; he didn't want a bridge here, ever; he liked this little canyon, which he had never seen before, the name of which he didn't even know, quite well enough as it was. Hayduke knelt and wrote a message in the sand to all highway construction contractors: 'Go home.' " This canyon is not Yosemite, or even Hetch Hetchy—there is no way to rally a crowd to its defense by virtue of its splendor or its opportunities for recreation. It has no human use. If the road isn't built, no one will ever come here. This canyon can only be paved over or be left alone to no constructive end. Abbey's radicalism was that he chose the latter.

THE EUROPEAN GREEN PARTIES, the California versions of Eastern religions, the animal rights movement have all adapted parts of these ideas in recent years. But they've usually tied them up with other notions—socialism, say, or enlightenment. At least in its philosophy, the small but rapidly growing American environmental group Earth First! provides one of the purest examples of putting the rest of creation ahead of exclusively human concerns.

A decade ago Dave Foreman was wearing a suit and tie and working in Washington as chief lobbyist for the Wilderness Society. His thinking, though, was evolving in the same direction as Abbey's. "The whole time I'd been in Washington I'd been radical philosophically—I believed in wilderness for its own sake. But for a long time I'd believed the best way to get more wilderness was to be reasonable, to take Republican politicians to lunch." The Sagebrush Rebellion—the protests in the late 1970s by Western miners, ranchers, and timber barons led by men like James Watt who claimed that the small gains of environmentalists were too much—convinced him otherwise. "It made me realize we were fighting for crumbs under the table. I guess I came to the conclusion that the industrial empire was a cancer on the earth and that saving some dinky recreational areas was not enough. That we had to offer a fundamental challenge to Western civilization."

Earth First!—the group Foreman formed with a few friends when he left Washington and the Wilderness Society—is one of a few fledgling attempts to translate the philosophical radicalism of a Muir or an Abbey into action. Its motto is "No compromise in defense of Mother Earth," and its symbol is the monkey wrench. The group has grown quickly in the West, partly because of this tough image. Its journal, for instance, includes tips for sabotage, or "eco-defense," helpful hints that go well beyond Hayduke's level of expertise. When disabling heavy machinery, for instance, sugar is completely passé. Rock-polishing grit, mixed in a ratio of four parts motor oil to one part silicon carbide, works much better. Or perhaps the government has put a dirt airstrip in a wilderness area near you: if you go out at night and liberally salt the runway, chances are deer, elk, and moose will soon come along and paw it up, leaving large holes.

Such "ecotage" has worked in some places and backfired in others, often making life more difficult for conventional environmentalists. (Foreman was arrested late in the spring of 1989 on charges that he had conspired to cut down power lines. An FBI informant had apparently infiltrated Earth First! and Foreman charged that the government was attempting to destroy the group.) Indisputably, Earth First!'s confrontational tactics have earned the group far more publicity than it could have gotten any other way.

But all the attention paid to the sabotage has usually overshadowed the group's message, which is at least as radical as its methods. It wants a different world, where roads are torn out to create vast new wildernesses, where most development ceases, and where much of man's imprint on the earth is slowly erased. Earth First! and the few other groups like it have a purpose, and that purpose is defense of the wild, the natural, the nonhuman.

The first time I heard Foreman speak, it was in a Sacramento, California, church basement. He began by ripping off his button-down shirt to reveal a black T-shirt with the raised monkey wrench emblazoned on it. He told of his days in Washington: "From my Wilderness Society experience, I began to wonder, Why preserve a wilderness area? Because it's a nice place to go and relax? Because you can make pretty books of pictures of it? To protect a watershed? No. You protect a river because it's a river. For its own sake. Because it has a right to exist by itself. The grizzly bear in Yellowstone Park has as much right to her life as any one of us has to our life," Foreman told the crowd. "Each of you is an animal and you should be proud of it."

"There are fundamental problems of philosophy at the root of all of this," insists Foreman. Most environmental groups discuss the need to "balance continued economic growth" with the "protection for future generations of our natural heritage." Foreman says, "I have really thought about it and tried to look for good news, for signs that reform will work. And I have come to the belief that the flaw is fundamental, unreformable. We can have big wildernesses, and we can reintroduce extirpated species, but unless the fact that there are way too many people on the earth is dealt with, unless the idea that the world is a resource for us to use is dealt with, unless humans can find their way home again, then the problems will continue."

Foreman and others have a name for this idea of people "finding their way home"—"deep ecology." In contrast to conventional, or "shallow," ecology, which basically accepts the anthropocentric worldview of the industrial state and merely wants to reform it—to turn mankind into better stewards—deep ecologists, in Foreman's words, "ask harder questions, such as: Where are we from? What is our relationship to the rest of the world? Are we really at the apex of evolution?" Their answers, not sand in the gas tanks of bulldozers, constitute "the fundamental challenge to Western civilization."

And, because we are all products and beneficiaries of that civilization, such ideas are a horrible challenge, even to those who think of themselves as environmentalists. When the *Nation* magazine printed an article outlining some of the tenets of deep ecology, it drew many angry letters. Deep ecology takes "the side of nature over culture," complained an "ecofeminist" named Ynestra King in a long missive, and in so doing it overlooks "the structures of entrenched economic and political power within society." Foreman "and his macho crowd . . . represent nothing more than the Daniel Boone mentality in ecological drag," she said. But to her the real problem is that Earth First! and deep ecology represent a "deep insensitivity to human suffering."

And in a profound way she is right. It is an intensely disturbing idea that man should not be the master of all, that other suffering might be just as important. And that individual suffering—animal or human—might be less important than the suffering of species, ecosystems, the planet. It is disturbing in a way that an idea like, say, Marxism is not. It is not all that radical to talk about who is going to own the factories, at least compared with the question of whether there are going to *be* factories.

IN SOUTHWEST OREGON, in the country above Grants Pass, the Rogue and the Illinois rivers dash toward the Pacific through steep valleys, most of them part of the Siskiyou National Forest. A portion of this land has been officially designated the Kalmiopsis Wilderness, in honor of a rare orchid found only within its borders. A few years ago, though, there were still at least 160,000 acres without roads, without logging—and without protection. It was here that some of Foreman's and Abbey's followers were mounting a small part of this "fundamental challenge to Western civilization."

The land harbors bear, white-tailed deer, Roosevelt elk, wolf, wolverine, bobcat, mountain lion, mink, otter, beaver, and osprey; in the cold streams salmon and steelhead spawn. Most important of all, the area supports a mighty stand of old-growth forest. Old-growth, or climax, forest is a rare sight nowadays in the United States, where all but 2 or 3 percent of the commercially suitable forests have been cut at least once. It's not simply that the trees of a climax forest are old; there are young trees, too, and dead, rotting trees—an endlessly complex ecosystem. But to a lumberman trees past their peak growth years are "decadent"; he wants to chop them down and install row-planted, single-species, "even-aged" plantations. "Trees are a renewable resource," the "forest products" industry proclaims, but old growth is not. Its snags and broken crowns and its remote, unroaded inaccessibility make it crucial habitat for certain species; Oregon's spotted owl will not live elsewhere, for instance.

The Forest Service decided, as it usually does, to allow loggers on this land—public land, which is owned by every American, as is half the land in the western United States. Its decision made some sense in the usual way of looking at things. There were loggers in the valley who needed work. The world needs a lot of wood. (You're holding a branch or two in your hands right now.) And it's rugged country, so no one much gets back there. It's like the canyon in Abbey's book: Why save it? To make it possible for loggers to reach the prime stands the Forest Service proposed to build, with taxpayer funds, a road along the shoulder of Bald Mountain into the heart of the area. The road would forever end this land's chance of being preserved as wilderness and it would fill the valleys it crossed with trucks and noise and men.

I walked the half-finished Bald Mountain Road with a local man, Steve Marsden. Actually, we walked not on the road but on a ridge trail that runs about ten feet above it. A judge had ordered Marsden to stay clear of the road itself, a ruling he was willing to violate but not until it was really necessary. Anyway, it was much prettier up on the path, which sometimes wound off into the woods. An hour or so into our hike we stopped to rest. From where we sat we could see several Douglas firs, a Brewer spruce, a distant relation of the American chestnut called the chincopia, a number of sugar pine, an eastern white pine, a grand fir, a shasta red fir, a knobcone pine, and a rare tree called the Port Orford cedar that has been wiped out in much of the surrounding area by a fungus that rolls in on the logging trucks. "This may be the most diverse conifer forest in the world," Marsden said. "A square mile contains seventeen cone-bearing species. It's at a low elevation, so during the last Ice Age it didn't glaciate. It doesn't have the spectacular views like the Sierras or the Cascades, but from a biological standpoint it may be the most valuable forest in the country." Valuable not so much to man—the bark of the Port Orford cedar probably doesn't contain any cancer-curing compound. Valuable only to itself.

Marsden knows the territory well. "I was a road engineer for the Forest Service. I did reconnaissance work for roads where there weren't any. I was out in primo territory all the time. And I told myself I was just doing my job. That's how I thought, and that's how a lot of guys think. A lot of the guys I worked with agree that the Forest Service is screwed up, but they sort of dissociate themselves." Marsden eventually disdissociated himself; he simply couldn't stand the way the Forest Service looked at the woods. "Wilderness rubs the professional foresters the wrong way," he said. "You go to school all those years, you want to manage." Until a judge stopped them, they were spraying Agent Orange–like herbicides from helicopters to keep down the shrubs. "To the Forest Service it's like growing corn—you weed, you fertilize, you plant all the same thing." And when it's time to harvest, you clear-cut, stripping every single tree from a plot of land. "A clear-cut is worse than a forest fire," said Marsden. "At least with a fire there's some residual left. Most of the biomass doesn't leave the area to make a split-level in San Diego."

When the Bald Mountain Road was first proposed, Marsden got together with other local environmentalists to try to save the road-less area. A letter from one of them alerted Earth First! and soon

Mike Roselle, who with Foreman helped found the group, arrived in Grants Pass. He learned that there was much opposition to the road but that not many people were willing to put their bodies on the line; finally, two locals—Steve Marsden was one of them—agreed to go with him and lie down in front of the bulldozers.

This was no antinuclear rally. This was fifteen miles of twisting dirt road from the nearest town, with no reporters around to watch. And the opponents were not policemen trained to arrest people but heavy-equipment operators trained to rip up the woods. "We were shivering, scared to death," said Roselle. "There was a friend of ours with a camera pretending to be media, because we hoped that might deter them a little bit. We didn't know if we'd get six months or ten years. We asked the lawyers, and they just said, 'Don't do it.' Well, on the first day we introduced ourselves to the construction workers. We said it's nothing against you guys personally—we just don't like this road, and we want to stop it. The next day we stopped it." They were arrested, jailed, released, and they returned, this time with more accomplices. By summer's end there were as many as forty-five blockaders; they avoided Forest Service roadblocks by hiking in at night along the path that Marsden and I were following.

Such demonstrations are nothing new, of course; people have sat down in front of bulldozers since bulldozers were invented. But the argument—the explicit idea that big isolated chunks of the planet have an intrinsic importance that outweighs any of man's plans for them—is still rare. In any event, the protests worked, slowing construction for several months, until lawyers could win an injunction against the work. That is not the same thing as changing civilization, but then Rome didn't decline and fall in a single day.

WHEN I WAS TRAVELING the West a few years ago, interviewing these people and seeing the scenery around them, I admired their guts and understood a lot that they said. But I am an easterner; I didn't have any intuitive sense of what it meant to live in a place where battles over the land are constant. Back east, and in most of Europe, people have pretty much figured out the areas they will settle and control, which is just about everywhere. The few areas leftover—such as, for instance, the Adirondacks—are more or less protected, by law and by tradition. So, while I believed once I saw the site that the Bald Mountain Road was a bad idea (it would be hard for anyone without a cash interest, I think, to stand in that cathedral forest and decide to cut it down), I didn't see stopping it as a matter of life and death. All the talk about fundamental challenges to industrial civilization struck me as a trifle overblown, loopy.

But I've since learned more about the greenhouse effect. Now, with the atmosphere changing thanks to our way of life, ideas like deep ecology interest me for more than philosophical reasons— they seem at least plausible. That is, they are extreme solutions, but we live in an extreme time. I cannot imagine any change more extreme than the change from four billion years of nature to year one of artifice. If industrial civilization is ending nature, it is not utter silliness to talk about ending—or, at least, transforming—industrial civilization.

We've taken, as individuals and as nations, certain moderate steps in the past few decades—created wildernesses, reintroduced eagles where they had been wiped out, cut the lead in our gasoline, and so on. But the world didn't seem to be demanding basic changes in the way we lived. Perhaps now it is. Perhaps what was for Thoreau an aesthetic choice is for us a practical one; perhaps the choice is, figuratively, if not literally, between endless rows of headless chickens and some new, very much more humble way of life.

There have been other such dramatic moments in modern history—moments when a sea change seemed possible. Before the Depression socialism looked like a preposterously radical idea to most Americans, something to be either hunted down and squashed or discussed in abstract and philosophical terms.

And then came the crash, and it no longer seemed a priori ridiculous. As it turned out, Franklin Roosevelt appeared with what was probably a better, less radical solution: Social Security instead of socialism. But alternatives, simply because they are more moderate, are not always more correct. It could be that this idea of a humbler world, or some idea like it, is both radical and necessary, in the way that cutting off a leg can be both radical and necessary.

A HALF HOUR'S HIKE brings my dog and me to the top of the hill behind my house. I know the hill well by now, each gully and small creek, each big rock, each opening around the edges. I know the places where the deer come, and the coyotes after them. It is no Bald Mountain, no unlogged virgin forest with trees ten feet around, but it is a deep and quiet and lovely place all the same.

Only the thought of what will happen as the new weather kicks in darkens my view: the trees dying, the hillside unable to hold its soil against the rainfall, the gullies sharpening, the deer looking for ever-scarcer browse. And, finally, the scrub and brush colonizing the slopes, clinging to what soil remains. Either that or the cemetery rows of perfect, heat-tolerant genetically improved pines.

From the top of the hill, if I stand on a certain ledge, I can see my house down below, white against the hemlocks. I can see my whole material life—the car, the bedroom, the chimney above the stove. I like that life, I like it enormously. But a choice seems unavoidable. Either that life down there changes, perhaps dramatically, or this life all around me up here changes—passes away.

That is a terrible choice. Two years ago, when I got married, my wife and I had the standard hopes and dreams, and their fulfillment seemed not so far away. We love to travel; we had set up our lives so that work wouldn't tie us down. Our house is nice and big—it seemed only a matter of time before it would fill with the racket of children.

As the consequences of the greenhouse effect have become clearer to us, though, we've started to prune and snip our desires. Instead of taking long vacation trips in the car, we ride our bikes on the road by the house. Instead of building a wood-fired hot tub for the backyard (the closest I've ever come to real decadence), we installed exciting new thermal-pane windows. Most of our other changes have been similarly small. We heat with our wood, and we try to keep the house at 55 degrees. We drive much less frequently; we shop twelve times a year, and there are weeks when we do not venture out at all. Though I'm a lousy gardener, I try to grow more and more of our food.

Still, those are the easy things, especially if you live in the country. And they're as much pleasure as sacrifice. It may be icy in most of the house but it's warm cuddled by the stove. I like digging in the garden, though it makes me more nervous than it did when it was pure hobby: if a storm knocks down a tomato plant, I feel slightly queasy. If we don't travel great distances and constantly see new sights, we have come to know the few square miles around us in every season and mood.

But there are harder changes, too, places where the constricting world has begun to bind and pinch. It is dawning on me and my wife that the world we inhabit is not the world we grew up in, the world where our hopes and dreams were formed. That responsibility may mean something new and sad. In other words, we try very hard not to think about how much we'd like a baby.

And it may take even more. Sometimes I stand on top of the hill and wonder if someday we'll need to move away, perhaps live closer to other people. Probably that would be more energy efficient. Would I love the woods enough to leave them behind? I stand up there and look out over the mountain to the east and the lake to the south and the rippling wilderness knolls stretching off to the west— and to the house below with the line of blue smoke trailing out of the chimney. One world or the other will have to change.

AND IF IT IS the human world that changes—if this humbler idea begins to win out—what will the planet look like? Will it appeal only to screwballs, people who thrive on a monthly shower and no steady income?

It's hard to draw a detailed picture—it's so much easier to picture the defiant future, for it is merely the extension of our current longings. I've spent my whole life wanting more, so it's hard for me to imagine "less" in any but a negative way. But that imagination is what counts. Changing the way we think is at the heart of the question. If it ever happens, the actions will follow.

For example, to cope with the greenhouse problem, people may need to install more efficient washing machines. But if you buy such a machine and yet continue to feel that it's both your right and your joy to have a big wardrobe, then the essential momentum of our course won't be broken. For big wardrobes imply a world pretty much like our own, where people pile up possessions, and where human desire is the only measure that counts. Even if such a world somehow licks the greenhouse effect, it will still fall in a second for, say, the cornucopia of genetic engineering. On the other hand, you could slash your stock of clothes to a comfortable (or even uncomfortable) minimum and then chip in with your neighbors to buy a more efficient washing machine to which you would lug your dirty laundry. If we reached that point—the point where great closetfuls of clothes seemed slightly absurd, *unnatural*—then we might have begun to climb down from the tottering perch where we currently cling.

"Absurd" and "unnatural" are different from "wrong" or "immoral." This is not a moral argument. There are plenty of good reasons having to do with aesthetics or whimsy to own lots of sharp clothes. (And many more and much better reasons to, say, drive cars or raise large families.) But those reasons may be outweighed by the burden that such desires place on the natural world. And if we could see that clearly, then our thinking might change of its own accord.

In this particular example, the thinking is more radical than the action. If we decided against huge wardrobes (which is to say, against a whole way of looking at ourselves) and against every family's owning a washer (which is to say, against a pervasive individual consumerism), then taking your clothes down the street to wash them would be the most obvious idea in the world. If people *hadn't* changed their minds about such things, these would be obnoxious developments—you'd need to employ secret police to make sure they weren't washing in private. It wouldn't be worth it, and it wouldn't work. But if we had changed our minds, our current ways of life might soon seem as bizarre as the six thousand shoes of Imelda Marcos.

It's normal to imagine that this humbler world would resemble the past. Simply because the atmosphere was cleaner a century ago, though, there's no call to forget all that's been developed since. My wife and I just acquired a fax machine, for instance, on the premise that it makes for graceful, environmentally sound communication—an advanced way to do with less. But if communication prospered in a humbler world, transportation might well wither, as people began to live closer not only to their work but to their food supply. Oranges all year round—oranges at any season in the northern latitudes—might prove ambitious beyond our means, just as the tropics might have to learn to do without apples. We—or, at least, our grandchildren—might come to use the "appropriate technologies" of "sustainable development" that we urge on peasants through organizations like the Peace Corps—bicycle-powered pumps, solar cookstoves, and so on. And, as in a less-developed country (a phrase that would probably turn into a source of some pride), more Westerners might find their work connected directly with their supper. That is to say, they would farm, which begins to sound a little quaint, a little utopian.

But conventional utopian ideas are not much help, either. Invariably they are designed to advance human happiness, which is found to be suffering as the result of crowding or stress or lack of meaningful work or not enough sex or too much sex. Machinery is therefore abolished, or cities abandoned, or families legislated against—but it's all in the name of man. Dirt under your nails will make you happier!

The humbler world I am describing is just the opposite. Human happiness would be of secondary importance. Perhaps it would be best for the planet if we all lived not in kibbutzes or on Jeffersonian farms, but crammed into a few huge cities like so many ants. I doubt a humbler world would be one big happy Pennsylvania Dutch colony. Certain human sadnesses might diminish; other human sadnesses would swell. But that would be beside the point. This is not an attempt at a utopia—as I said, I'm happy now. It's a stab at something else—an "atopia," perhaps—where our desires are not the engine.

The ground rules for such an atopia would be few enough. We would have to conquer the desire to grow in numbers; the human population would need to get gradually smaller, though how much smaller is an open question. Some deep ecologists say the human population shouldn't exceed a hundred million, others a billion or two—roughly our population a century ago. And those people would need to use less in the way of resources—not just oil, but wood and water and chemicals and even land itself. Those are the essentials. But they are practical rules, not moral ones. Within them, a thousand cultures—vegetarian and hunter, communal and hermitic—could still exist.

A pair of California professors, George Sessions and Bill Devall, listed what they saw as some of the principles of deep ecology in a book (*Deep Ecology*) they published several years ago. Although the work shows its West Coast origins at times (there is some discussion of how this philosophy could give us "joyous confidence to dance with the sensuous harmonies discovered through spontaneous, playful intercourse with the rhythms of our bodies, the rhythms of flowing water"), it is frank about the sharp contrast between the current worldview and their proposed replacement: instead of material and economic growth, "elegantly simple" material needs; instead of consumerism, "doing with enough." It is frank, too, in its acknowledgment that deep ecology—that humility—is an infant philosophy, with many questions yet to be asked, much less answered: Exactly how much is enough? Or, what about poor people?

Those are hard questions—but perhaps not beyond our imagination. When we decided that accumulation and growth were our economic ideals, we invented wills and lending at interest and puritanism and supersonic aircraft. Why would we come up with ideas less powerful in an all-out race to do with less?

The difficulty is almost certainly more psychological than intellectual—less that we can't figure out major alterations in our way of life than that we simply don't want to. Even if our way of life has destroyed nature and endangered the planet, it is so hard to imagine living in any other fashion. The people whose lives may point the way—Thoreau, say, or Gandhi—we dismiss as exceptional, a polite way of saying there is no reason we should be expected to go where they pointed. The challenge they presented with the physical examples of their lives is much more subversive than anything they wrote or said: if they could live those simple lives, it's no use saying we could not. I could, I suppose, get by on half the money I currently spend. A voluntary simplification of life-styles is not beyond our abilities, but it is probably outside our de-sires.

AND OUR DESIRES COUNT. Nothing is necessarily going to force us to live humbly; we are free to chance the other, defiant route and see what happens. The only thing we absolutely must do is cut back immediately on our use of fossil fuels. That is not an option; we need to do it in order to choose any other future. But there is no certainty we must simultaneously cut back on our material desires—not if we're willing to live in a world ever more estranged from na-ture. Both the defiant and the humble alternatives offer ways to adapt to the greenhouse effect, this total upheaval. They present us with a choice.

The obvious objection to this choice is that it does not exist: that man always pushes restlessly ahead, that it's inevitable, biological, part of "human nature." That is a cop-out, at least intellectually—that is, it may be true, but those of us who have thought about the question still have the moral burden of making a choice. Anyway, there are examples of civilizations, chiefly Eastern ones, that by choice spent centuries almost suspended in time. I *can* imagine a world in which we decide not to conduct genetic experiments or to build new dams, just as a few people in the late nineteenth century began to imagine forests that were not logged and so preserved the Adirondacks. As I said, I'm not certain what that world would look like. Probably it would have to develop an enormously powerful so-cial taboo against "progress" of the defiant kind—a religious or quasi-religious horror at the thought of "improved chickens" and large families. And I'm not saying I see the path from here to any of the possible theres; my point is merely that, for the purpose of ar-gument, I can imagine such a world. Possession of a certain tech-nology imposes on us no duty to use it.

A second obvious objection is that perhaps we needn't decide now, that surely we can leave it for some future generation to figure out. That is an attractive idea and a traditional one; we have been putting off this particular question since at least 1864, when George

Perkins Marsh, the first modern environmentalist, wrote that by our tree cutting and swamp draining we were "breaking up the floor and wainscotting and doors and window-frames of our dwelling for fuel to warm our bodies."

I have tried to explain, though, why it cannot be put off any longer. We just happen to be living at the moment when the carbon dioxide has increased to an intolerable level. We just happen to be alive at the moment when if nothing is done before we die the world's tropical rain forests will become a brown girdle around the planet that will last for millennia. It's simply our poor luck; it might have been nicer to have been born in 1890 and died in 1960, confident that everything was looking up. We just happen to be living in the decade when genetic engineering is acquiring a momentum that will soon be unstoppable. The comforting idea that we could decide to use such technology to, in the words of Lewis Thomas, cure "most of the unsolved diseases on society's agenda" and then not use it to straighten trees or grow giant trout seems implausible to me: we're already doing those things.

One needs, obviously, to be wary of millennialism. And it's perhaps not fair that those of us currently alive should have to deal with these developments. On the other hand, it wasn't fair that our fathers had to go fight Hitler. The American Methodist Church has just adopted a new hymnal, and, along with the usual wrangles over sexism and militarism and so on, there was a dispute over a marvelous Civil War–era hymn by James Russell Lowell. "Once to Every Man and Nation," it begins, "comes the moment to decide, / In the strife of truth with falsehood, for the good or evil side. / Some great cause, God's new messiah, offering each the bloom or blight, / And the choice goes by forever, / 'Twixt the darkness and the light." The hymnal committee reportedly decided against the tune on the grounds that it was unsound theology—that once was not enough, that it was never too late for a person to reform. But this was one of Martin Luther King's favorite hymns, and in terms of public policy, if not personal salvation, I fear it may be all too true.

OF THESE TWO PATHS which one will we choose? It's impossible to know for certain, but there's no question but that the momentum of our age ceaselessly hurries us ahead, making it horribly difficult to choose the humble path and incredibly easy to follow the defiant one.

I have a neighbor, a logger whom I'll call Jim Franklin. Jim honestly believes that the cause of acid rain in the Adirondacks is "too many trees," the result of environmentalists' setting too much land aside as wilderness. He has worked out a theory, something about the mat of pine needles accumulating on the ground, which I can't begin to repeat even though I have heard it several times. "I told it to the forest ranger and he just looked at me," says Jim, as if this were proof of the conspiracy. We believe things because we have a need to believe them. (That is not a novel insight, I realize.) Jim wants to log for economic reasons and for reasons that might be described as psychological or cultural, and he has constructed an idea to support his desire. But it is not a lie: he believes it to be true. Muir, on his thousand-mile stroll to the Gulf of Mexico, met a man in a particularly backward section of North Carolina who said to him: "I believe in Providence. Our fathers came into these valleys, got the richest of them, and skimmed the cream of the soil. The worn-out ground won't yield no roasting ears now. But the Lord foresaw this state of affairs and prepared something else for us. And what is it? Why, He meant us to bust open these copper mines and gold mines, so that we may have money to buy the corn we cannot raise." Though this argument has its obvious weaknesses, it is immensely appealing, just as the thought of a new genetically engineered cornucopia is appealing: it means we wouldn't have to change.

And we don't want to change. Jim wants to log as he always has. I want to be able to drive as I always have and go on living in the large house I live in and so on. The tidal force of biology continues to govern us, even when we realize (as no lemming can) that we're doing something stupid. This genetic inheritance from millions of years ago when it did make sense to grow and expand can't simply be shrugged off.

And the opposing forces are so weak. In a curious way, for example, some environmentalists have made it easier for people to ignore global threats. In the late 1960s and early 1970s, a spate of horror books came out—books filled with the direst predictions. "At the current rate of population increase, there will be a billion billion people on the face of the earth, or seventeen hundred for every square mile," wrote Paul Ehrlich. "Projecting this farther into the future, in about two thousand or three thousand years people would weigh more than the earth; in five thousand years everything in the visible universe would be converted into people, and their expansion would be at the speed of light." While this was technically true, it was also so unrealistic that we could safely ignore it. The greenhouse effect, he wrote, might raise ocean levels two hundred and fifty feet. "Gondola to the Empire State Building, anyone? he asked. "Lake Erie has died. . . . Lake Michigan will soon follow it into extinction."

But that didn't happen. Lake Erie rose again—still sick, of course, but not dead. The oil crisis eased and then turned into an oil glut. The greenhouse effect could realistically raise the sea level ten feet, which is plenty bad enough but sounds like nothing next to two hundred and fifty. With every unfulfilled apocalyptic projection, our confidence in the environmentalists has waned, our belief that we'll muddle through been bolstered.

We'll look for almost any reason not to change our attitudes; the inertia of the established order is powerful. If we can think of a plausible, or even implausible, reason to discount environmental warnings, we will. If a solitary scientist says, as S. Fred Singer did in a recent issue of *The Wall Street Journal*, that the greenhouse effect is a "mixture of fact and fancy," we read it to mean that the whole business is nonsense. And if we can imagine a plausible reason to believe that it will all be okay—if someone tells us that we can "manage" the planet, for instance—the temptation is to believe him. In 1980, when Ronald Reagan ran for the presidency, he made his shrillest attacks on the idea that we might be living in an "age of limits." This notion, perhaps the first necessary recognition on the road to a new relationship with the earth, a first baby step on a thousand-mile journey toward deep ecology, had gained some small currency with Carter administration officials. But Reagan attacked it mercilessly. Occasionally, as when he announced that trees pollute, he got in a little trouble. But the country forgave him, because it wanted to believe him—wanted to believe that, even though the shadows seemed to be lengthening, it was "morning in America." Unfortunately, optimism didn't aid the ozone layer.

IN VERY LARGE MEASURE, our helplessness is a problem of affluence. The perceptive essayist (and farmer) Wendell Berry once remarked that because the agricultural life "made serious demands upon the human in return for benefits given, the industrial age was invented to avoid the return due for benefits incurred." Now that most of us in the West are several generations away from that earlier way of life, our sense of entitlement is almost impossible to shake. That is why the energy crisis was so interesting: for a brief moment, it actually unnerved us. We carpooled—we gave up exclusive control of the radio dial. But it seems to have unnerved us only on an individual basis. We were afraid we wouldn't be able to find gas, and upset that it cost so much. I remember thinking a few years ago, when for the first time in my motoring life the numbers on the gallon dial spun quicker than the numbers on the dollars dial, and Texaco started handing out water glasses, that this would be the real test of the meaning of the gas crisis. If people had perceived it as a warning of the earth's fragility, of its essentially finite nature, then perhaps they would keep driving Toyotas when the price of gas came down.

In the summer of 1988, a month after the Senate testimony on fossil fuels and the greenhouse effect, in the middle of the August heat wave, on the same day that *The New York Times* ran a huge piece titled "The Planet Strikes Back," the paper's front page featured a story on the hot new cars. "Car Makers of the World Revive Horsepower Race," it declared, citing the decision of Corvette to increase its power from 245 horsepower to a whopping 400, and the long waiting lists for a Ferrari capable of beating two hundred miles per hour. "Now, with fuel cheap, a fast car has again become a success symbol," it concluded. "Performance is a hot topic," the advertising executive in charge of the Dodge account told reporters. "People have money and they want to get back to driving the way it used to be—fun."

As a result of this reversion to form, the federal government that fall decided to relax fuel-economy laws. Since 1976 American car builders had been required to raise the average fuel efficiencies of new cars. By 1988 new cars were supposed to be averaging 27.5 miles per gallon. But the companies, citing consumer demand, said they would have to limit production of their biggest cars to meet the overall standard. Cadillac had added nine inches to its Sedan DeVille, for instance, and Buick had stuck nearly a foot on the 1989 Riviera—these were the cars people wanted. And so the Department of Transportation decided in October 1988, just weeks after the latest EPA report on the need to reduce fossil-fuel use, to cut the figure back to 26.5 miles per gallon.

Our tentative moves toward alternative forms of energy seem to have been just as halfhearted. Through the mid-1980s the United States was the world's largest market for solar collectors. Then, in 1986, as oil prices fell, the federal government eliminated tax credits for putting the things on your roof. Sales volume dropped 70 percent, according to the Worldwatch Institute; twenty-eight thousand of the industry's thirty thousand employees lost their jobs.

The point is, it's easier, and thus "more fun," to use oil for almost everything. Raking leaves, for instance. By 1987 Americans alone had paid more than a hundred million dollars to buy electric leaf blowers—machines that blow leaves around a yard, thereby replacing the rake. Never mind that they make a horrible racket, or that when you use one the chance of daydreaming disappears—and certainly never mind the thought that they give off greenhouse gases. "Blowers are far more efficient, because you're harnessing gasoline, not muscles," said John F. Cockerill of the New York Turf and Landscape Association in a recent article. "It's a lot less tiring." Was Wendell Berry exaggerating when he said that the Industrial Revolution was an attempt to avoid the return due for our benefits? After only a hundred and fifty years of our addiction to oil, we can barely comprehend change—it seems so scary. It seems like work, and like being cramped in a little car.

Van Wyck Brooks, the historian of literature, contended that most aristocratic Southerners felt the abolition of slavery to be both "right and necessary," but they opposed it nonetheless. "The economic life of the South was founded on slavery, and the question seemed too difficult to solve." I think the analogy is not overdrawn: we can engage in newspaper debates about the need for new national energy policies and so on, but our individual personal economies rely so heavily on the cheap labor provided by oil that change, and especially the radical change to something like the deep ecological model, almost can't be conceived. Dr. Chauncey Starr, who is the president emeritus of the Electric Power Research Institute, an industry arm, pointed out recently that cutting in half the carbon dioxide emissions from electric power plants in the United States would delay a greenhouse warming only a year or two. "What would you be willing to pay for that?" he asked.

We flatter ourselves that we think of the future. Politicians are always talking about our children, our grandchildren, and, as individuals, we do think about them, but in the same way that we think about ourselves. We lay aside money for them, or land. But we do not really think of grandchildren in general. "Future generations do not vote; they have no political or financial power; they cannot challenge our decisions," said a perceptive introduction to the United Nations report on *Our Common Future*. Future generations depend on us, but not vice versa. "We act as we do because we can get away with it."

IT IS EASY to lampoon electric leaf blowers. But this paralysis of affluence is dwarfed by the paralysis of poverty that afflicts most of the world. It's not just Westerners, for instance, who want cars. In 1985, according to the researcher Michael Renner, only a little more than 1 percent of the population of the Third World owned an automobile, compared with 40 percent in the Western industrialized countries. "Yet the lure of owning a private passenger car—

and the status, mobility, and better life its possession seems to promise—seem irresistible everywhere on the globe," Renner went on to say. "As soon as income allows, many people accord high priority to buying a car." As a result, both China and India have "embarked on policies that seek to emulate the motorized transport system of the industrial West."

It does not require much imagination to foresee the results for the atmosphere if, someday, the same percentage of Kenyans— far less than of Indians or Chinese—as Germans drive cars. Or if even half the proportion, or a quarter. In general, the average sub-Saharan uses one-eightieth as much energy as the average Belgian or Finn or American. Thus, in the words of a United Nations report, "any realistic global energy scenario must provide for substantially increased primary energy use by developing countries."

The thought that people living in poverty, be it desperate poverty or just depressing poverty, will curb their desire for a marginally better life simply because of something like the greenhouse effect is, of course, absurd. A cyclone killed three hundred thousand Bangladeshis in 1970. As soon as the water drained, people resettled the land. The willingness to take this sort of risk testifies to a hunger that can only increase if, as expected, the country's population doubles. They are going to moderate their "lifestyles," pare down their "desires," in order to avoid releasing carbon dioxide? The subsistence farmers of the tropics, with no alternative method for feeding their families, will cease their slash-and-burn agriculture?

This overwhelming poverty, though, affects the rich as well as the poor, in that it keeps all discussions of solutions muted. On the one hand, it is inconceivable, at least this side of some genetically engineered bounty, that the peoples of the developing world could ever enjoy a standard of living like ours; there is simply not enough plastic and copper and so on to go around. If by 2025 energy consumption in every country reached the current levels of the industrialized countries, it would mean a load five and a half times as big as the present environmentally unsupportable one. On the other hand, it is politically—and humanly—impossible to say that the poor should be condemned to live without while we live with.

Since environmentalists cannot alleviate poverty by increasing the amount of goods, one would logically expect them to advocate a drastic redistribution of wealth. The environmentally sane standard of living for a population our current size would probably be somewhere between that of the average Englishman and of the average Ethiopian—each lives unreasonably. But this sort of talk would erode what support environmental concerns enjoy among the privileged. Do you want to use your car one-fifth as often so that five Ethiopians can drive theirs without damaging the air? Or even, assuming that you could double the efficiency of your car, do you want to drive half as much? Much easier to continue hoping that the pie is or will be large enough for all of us to have two slices; that way our enjoyment is impaired by neither limit nor guilt.

The most extreme counterargument—expressed by Robinson Jeffers in the advice "Be in nothing so moderate as in love of man"—sounds heartless because it is, especially coming from someone well fed and well housed like me. But it has certain virtues, such as intellectual honesty. In 1988, during the American summer heat, a *New York Times* editorial declared: "Sweltering through a 95-degree day is not a choice but yet another facet of poverty. If a civilized New York is a place in which everyone could come in from the cold, this torrid summer reminds us that it's also a place in which everyone could come in from the heat." A civilized New York—and, by extension, a civilized world, since an awful lot of places suffer 95-degree days—is a world in which poor people have air-conditioning. Nowhere does the editorialist suggest that all this new air-conditioning, by sucking up electricity, will increase the greenhouse effect, or that by releasing chlorofluorocarbons it will erode the ozone layer, though surely these would be greater catastrophes for the poor. And certainly he doesn't suggest that we might be better off, rich and poor, doing with less air-conditioning in an effort to save the atmosphere. This last is not some fantasy idea. People, after all, lived at the latitude of Manhattan for many centuries without benefit of air-conditioning. But because "civilized" New York has decided that it likes air-conditioning, it now feels the need to extend air-conditioning, if only in its imagination, to everyone. This will not cool off the sweating homeless in New

York, much less on the Indian subcontinent (where, if one were rationally allocating air conditioners, most of them would go). But it is the sort of thinking that could very well prevent anything major from ever being done here to curb fuel use. For example, S. Fred Singer, the greenhouse skeptic, writes that "drastically limiting the emission of carbon dioxide means cutting deeply into global energy use. But limiting economic growth condemns the poor, especially in the Third World, to continued poverty, if not outright starvation."

I am dubious about the actual depth of feeling for the Third World implied by such arguments—they mesh too conveniently with our desires. After all, limiting our standard of living and sharing our wealth would also help alleviate poverty, and an overheated, ozone-depleted world will probably be even crueler to the poor than to the rich. A humble path, in which the rich world meets the poor world halfway, seems to me to allow for far more justice than an ever-growing supply of air conditioners. We don't need to choose between cruelty and the greenhouse effect; there are more rational, if more difficult, ways to show our love of our fellow man. But I have no doubt at all about the power of humanist arguments like Singer's to stall effective action of any sort if we are reluctant to take such action in the first place.

THE INERTIA OF AFFLUENCE, the push of poverty, the soaring population—these and the other reasons listed earlier make me pessimistic about the chances that we will dramatically alter our ways of thinking and living, that we will turn humble in the face of our troubles.

A purely personal effort is, of course, just a gesture—a good gesture, but a gesture. The greenhouse effect is the first environmental problem we can't escape by moving to the woods. There are no personal solutions. There is no time to just decide we'll raise enlightened children and they'll slowly change the world. (When the problem was that someone might drop the Bomb, it perhaps made sense to bear and raise sane, well-adjusted children in the hope that they'd help prevent the Bomb from being dropped. But the problem now is precisely too many children, well adjusted or otherwise.)

We have to be the ones to do it, and simply driving less won't matter, except as a statement, a way to get other people—many other people—to drive less. *Most* people have to be persuaded, and persuaded quickly, to change.

But saying that something is difficult is not the same as saying it is impossible. After all, George Bush decided in the wake of the 1988 heat that he was an environmentalist. Margaret Thatcher, who in 1985 had linked environmental groups with other "subversives" as "the enemy within," found the religion at about the same time, after the death of the North Sea seals and the odyssey of the *Karin B*, the wandering toxic-waste barge. "Protecting the balance of nature," she said, is "one of the great challenges of the twentieth century."

I've been using the analogy of slavery throughout this discussion: we feel it our privilege (and we feel it a necessity) to dominate nature to our advantage, as whites once dominated blacks. When one method of domination seems to be ending—the reliance on fossil fuels, say—we cast about for another, like genetic tinkering, much as Americans replaced slavery with Jim Crow segregation. However, in my lifetime that official segregation ended. Through their courage, men and women like Martin Luther King and Fannie Lou Hamer managed to harness the majority's better qualities—idealism, love for one's neighbor—to transform the face of American society. Racism, it is true, remains virulent, but the majority of Americans have voted for legislators who passed laws—radical laws—mandating affirmative action programs. Out of some higher motive (and, of course, some base motives, such as the fear of black revolt), whites have sacrificed at least a little potential wealth and power. It would be wrong to say categorically that such a shift couldn't happen with regard to the environment—that a mixture of fear and the love for nature buried in most of us couldn't rise to the surface. Some small but significant steps have been taken. Los Angeles, for instance, recently enacted a series of laws to improve air quality that will change at least the edges of the lives of every resident. Los Angelenos will drive different cars, turn in their gas-powered lawn mowers, start their barbecues without lighter fluid.

Most of my hope, however, fades in the face of the uniqueness of the situation. As we have seen, nature is already ending, its passing quiet and accidental. And not only does its ending prevent us from returning to the world we previously knew, but it also, for two powerful reasons, makes any of the fundamental changes we've discussed even more unlikely than they might be in easier times. If the end of nature were still in the future, a preventable possibility, the equation might be different. But it isn't in the future—it's in the recent past, and the present.

THE END OF NATURE is a plunge into the unknown, fearful as much because it is unknown as because it might be hot or dry or whipped by hurricanes. This lack of security is the first reason that fundamental change will be much harder, for the changes we've been discussing—the deep ecology alternative, for instance—would make life even more unpredictable. One would have to begin to forgo the traditional methods of securing one's future—many children, many possessions, and so on. Jeremy Rifkin, in his book on genetic engineering, said there was still a chance we would choose to sacrifice "a measure of our own future security in order to represent the interests of the rest of the cosmos. . . . If we have been saving that spirit up for a propitious moment, then certainly now is the time for it to pour forth."

But now isn't the time—now, as the familiar world around us starts to change, is the moment when every threatened instinct will push us to scramble to preserve at least our familiar style of life. We can—and we may well—make the adjustments necessary for our survival. For instance, much of the early work in agricultural biotechnology has focused on inventing plants able to survive heat and drought. It seems the sensible thing to do—the way to keep life as "normal" as possible in the face of change. It leads, though, as I have said, to the second death of nature: the imposition of our artificial world in place of the broken natural one.

The rivers of the American Southwest, in particular the Colorado, provide a perfect example of this phenomenon. Though Ed

Abbey wrote about the entire Southwest, the one spot he kept returning to, the navel of his universe, was Glen Canyon dam. The dam, built a couple of decades ago near the Utah-Arizona line, is just upstream of the Grand Canyon. It backs up the waters of the Colorado into Lake Powell, a reservoir that rises and falls with the demand for hydroelectric power. The water covers Glen Canyon, a place so sweet Abbey called it "paradise"—and the description of his raft trip through the gorge shortly before the dam was finished makes the term sound weak, understated.

Since the degradation of this canyon stood in his mind for all human arrogance, its salvation would be the sign that man had turned the corner, begun the long trek back toward his proper station. (Blowing up the dam is the great aim of the Monkey Wrench Gang.) If we decide to take out the dam, it would signal many things, among them that perhaps the desert should not house huge numbers of people—that some should move, and others take steps to ensure smaller future generations. True, if we decide to take out the dam and the lake flowed away toward Mexico, it would "no doubt expose a drear and hideous scene: immense mud flats and whole plateaus of sodden garbage strewn with dead trees, sunken boats, the skeletons of long-forgotten, decomposing waterskiers," Abbey writes. "But to those who find the prospect too appalling, I say give nature a little time. In five years, at most in ten, the sun and wind and storms will cleanse and sterilize the repellent mess. The inevitable floods will soon remove all that does not belong within the canyons. Fresh green willow, box elder, and redbud will reappear; and the ancient drowned cottonwoods (noble monuments to themselves) will be replaced by young of their own kind. . . . Within a generation—thirty years—I predict the river and canyons will bear a decent resemblance to their former selves. Within the lifetime of our children Glen Canyon and the living river, heart of the canyonlands, will be restored to us. The wilderness will again belong to God, the people, and the wild things that call it home."

Such a vision is, of course, romantically unlikely under any circumstances. But the new insecurity that accompanies the end of nature makes it even more far-fetched. As we have seen, the projected increases in evaporation and decreases in rainfall in the Colorado watershed could cut flows along the river nearly in half. As a result, noted an EPA report, the reluctance in recent years to build big dams, for fear of environmental opposition, "may be re-evaluated in light of possible new demands for developed water under warm-dry climate change scenarios." Specifically, "climate change may create pressure to build the Animas-LaPlata and Narrows projects proposed for Colorado." In other words, where Abbey hoped for box elder and redbud more dams will bloom. The authors of *Gaia: An Atlas of Planet Management* are quite explicit about dam building. In a section on water conservation they put forth a lot of good ideas for fixing leaky mains and such, but they also sing the praises of damming rivers, a process that "can help satisfy a number of needs at once: it helps control flooding, provides the potential for generating hydropower, and stores water for a variety of purposes, including irrigation. The resulting reservoirs represent a multi-purpose resource, with potential for aquaculture and leisure activities." A flood-washed paradise of cottonwood or a "multi-purpose resource"—that is the choice, and it is not hard to guess, if the heat is on, what the voters of Arizona will demand.

I got a glimpse of this particular future a few years ago when I spent some time along the La Grande River, in sub-Arctic Quebec. It is barren land but beautiful—a tundra of tiny ponds and hummocks stretching to the horizon, carpeted in light-green caribou moss. There are trees—almost all black spruce, and all spindly, sparse. A number of Indians and Eskimos lived there—about the number the area could support. Then, a decade or so ago, Hydro-Quebec, the provincial utility, decided to exploit the power of the La Grande by building three huge dams along the river's 350-mile length. The largest, said the Hydro-Quebec spokesman, is the size of fifty-four thousand two-story houses or sixty-seven billion peas. Its spillway could carry the combined flow of all the rivers of Europe. And erecting it was a Bunyanesque task: eighteen thousand men carved the roads north through the tundra and poured the concrete. (Photos show the cooks stirring spaghetti sauce with canoe paddles.) On the one hand, this is a perfect example of "environmentally sound" energy generation; it produces an enormous amount of power without giving off so much as a whiff of any greenhouse gas. This is the sort of structure we'll be clamoring to build as the warming progresses.

But environmentally sound is not the same as natural. The dams have altered an area larger than Switzerland—the flow of the Caniapiscau River, for instance, has been partly reversed to provide more water for the turbines. In September 1984, at least ten thousand caribou drowned trying to cross the river during their annual migration. They were crossing at their usual spot, but the river was not its usual size; it was so swollen that many of the animals were swept forty-five miles downstream. Every good argument—the argument that fossil fuels cause the greenhouse effect; the argument that in a drier, hotter world we'll need more water; the argument that as our margin of security dwindles we must act to restore it— will lead us to more La Grande projects, more dams on the Colorado, more "management." Every argument—that the warmer weather and increased ultraviolet is killing plants and causing cancer; that the new weather is causing food shortages—will have us looking to genetic engineering for salvation. And with each such step we will move farther from nature.

AT THE SAME TIME—and this is the second kicker—the only real counterargument, the argument for an independent, eternal, eversweet nature, will grow ever fainter and harder to make. Why? Because nature, independent nature, is already ending. Fighting for it is like fighting for an independent Latvia except that it's harder, since the end of nature may be permanent. Take out Glen Canyon dam and let the Colorado run free, let the "inevitable floods" wash away the debris? But floods may be a thing of the past on the Colorado; the river may, in effect, be dammed at the source—in the clouds that no longer dump their freight on its upper reaches, and in the heat that evaporates the water that does fall.

If nature were about to end, we might muster endless energy to stave it off; but if nature has already ended, what are we fighting for? Before any redwoods had been cloned or genetically improved, one could understand clearly what the fight against such tinkering was about. It was about the idea that a redwood was somehow sacred, that its fundamental identity should remain beyond our control. But once that barrier has been broken, what is the fight about, then? It's not like opposing nuclear reactors or toxic waste dumps, each one of which poses new risks to new areas. This damage is to an idea, the idea of nature, and all the ideas that descend from it. It is not cumulative. Wendell Berry once argued that without a "fascination" with the wonder of the natural world "the energy needed for its preservation will never be developed"—that "there must be a mystique of the rain if we are ever to restore the purity of the rainfall." This makes sense when the problem is transitory—sulfur from a smokestack drifting over the Adirondacks. But how can there be a mystique of the rain now that every drop—even the drops that fall as snow on the Arctic, even the drops that fall deep in the remaining forest primeval—bears the permanent stamp of man? Having lost its separateness, it loses its special power. Instead of being a category like God—something beyond our control—it is now a category like the defense budget or the minimum wage, a problem we must work out. This in itself changes its meaning completely, and changes our reaction to it.

A few weeks ago, on the hill behind my house, I almost kicked the biggest rabbit I had ever seen. She had nearly finished turning white for the winter, and we stood there watching each other for a pleasant while, two creatures linked by curiosity. What will it mean to come across a rabbit in the woods once genetically engineered "rabbits" are widespread? Why would we have any more reverence or affection for such a rabbit than we would for a Coke bottle?

The end of nature probably also makes us reluctant to attach ourselves to its remnants, for the same reason that we usually don't choose friends from among the terminally ill. I love the mountain outside my back door—the stream that runs along its flank, and the smaller stream that slides down a quarter-mile mossy chute, and the place where the slope flattens into an open plain of birch and oak. But I know that some part of me resists getting to know it better—for fear, weak-kneed as it sounds, of getting hurt. If I knew as well as a forester what sick trees looked like, I fear I would see them everywhere. I find now that I like the woods best in winter, when it is harder to tell what might be dying. The winter woods might be perfectly healthy come spring, just as the sick friend, when she's sleeping peacefully, might wake up without the wheeze in her lungs.

Writing on a different subject, the bonds between men and women, Allan Bloom describes the difficulty of maintaining a committed relationship in an age when divorce—the end of that relationship—is so widely accepted: "The possibility of separation is already the fact of separation, inasmuch as people today must plan to be whole and self-sufficient and cannot risk interdependence." Instead of working to strengthen our attachments, our energies "are exhausted in preparation for independence." How much more so if that possible separation is definite, if that hurt and confusion is certain. I love winter best now, but I try not to love it too much, for fear of the January perhaps not so distant when the snow will fall as warm rain. There is no future in loving nature.

And there may not even be much past. Though Thoreau's writings grew in value and importance the closer we drew to the end of nature, the time fast approaches when he will be inexplicable, his notions less sensible to future men than the cave paintings are to us. Thoreau writes, on his climb up Katahdin, that the mountain "was vast, Titanic, and such as man never inhabits. Some part of the beholder, even some vital part, seems to escape through the loose grating of his ribs. . . . Nature has got him at a disadvantage, caught him alone, and pilfers him of some of his divine faculty. She does not smile on him as in the plains. She seems to say sternly, why came ye here before your time. This ground is not prepared for you." This sentiment describes perfectly the last stage of the relationship of man to nature—though we had subdued her in the low places, the peaks, the poles, the jungles still rang with her pure message. But what sense will this passage make in the years to come, when Katahdin, the "cloud factory," is ringed by clouds of man's own making? When the massive pines that ring its base have been genetically improved for straightness of trunk and "proper branch drop," or, more likely, have sprung from the cones of genetically improved trees that began a few miles and a few generations distant on some timber plantation? When the moose that ambles by is part of a herd whose rancher is committed to the enlightened, Gaian notion that "conservation and profit go hand in hand"?

Thoreau describes an afternoon of fishing at the mouth of Murch Brook, a dozen miles from the summit of Katahdin. Speckled trout "swallowed the bait as fast as we could throw in; and the finest specimens . . . that I have ever seen, the largest one weighing three pounds, were heaved upon the shore." He stood there to catch them as "they fell in a perfect shower" around him. "While yet alive, before their tints had faded, they glistened like the fairest flowers, the product of primitive rivers; and he could hardly trust his senses, as he stood over them, that these jewels should have swam away in that Aboljacknagesic water for so long, some many dark ages—these bright fluviatile flowers, seen of Indians only, made beautiful, the Lord only knows why, to swim there!" But through biotechnology we have already synthesized growth hormone for trout. Soon pulling them from the water will mean no more than pulling cars from an assembly line. We won't have to wonder why the Lord made them beautiful and put them there; we will have created them to increase protein supplies or fish-farm profits. If we want to make them pretty, we may. Soon Thoreau will make no sense. And when that happens, the end of nature—which began with our alteration of the atmosphere, and continued with the responses to our precarious situation of the "planetary managers" and the "genetic engineers"—will be final. The loss of memory will be the eternal loss of meaning.

IN THE END, I understand perfectly well that defiance may mean prosperity and a sort of security—that more dams will help the people of Phoenix, and that genetic engineering will help the sick, and that there is so much progress that can still be made against human misery. And I have no great desire to limit my way of life. If I thought we could put off the decision, foist it on our grandchildren, I'd be willing. As it is, I have no plans to live in a cave, or even an unheated cabin. If it took ten thousand years to get where we are, it will take a few generations to climb back down. But this could be the epoch when people decide at least to go no farther down the path we've been following—when we make not only the necessary technological adjustments to preserve the world from overheating but also the necessary mental adjustments to ensure that we'll never again put our good ahead of everything else's. This is the path I choose, for it offers at least a shred of hope for a living, eternal, meaningful world.

The reasons for my choice are as numerous as the trees on the hill outside my window, but they crystallized in my mind when I read a passage from one of the brave optimists of our managed future. "The existential philosophers—particularly Sartre—used to lament that man lacked an essential purpose," writes Walter Truett Anderson. "We find now that the human predicament is not quite so devoid of inherent purpose after all. To be caretakers of a planet, custodians of all its life forms and shapers of its (and our own) future is certainly purpose enough." This intended rallying cry depresses me more deeply than I can say. That is our destiny? To be "caretakers" of a managed world, "custodians" of all life? For that job security we will trade the mystery of the natural world, the pungent mystery of our own lives and of a world bursting with exuberant creation? Much better, Sartre's neutral purposelessness. But much better than that, another vision, of man actually living up to his potential.

As birds have flight, our special gift is reason. Part of that reason drives the intelligence that allows us, say, to figure out and master DNA, or to build big power plants. But our reason could also keep us from following blindly the biological imperatives toward endless growth in numbers and territory. Our reason allows us to conceive of our species as a species, and to recognize the danger that our growth poses to it, and to feel something for the other species we threaten. Should we so choose, we could exercise our reason to do what no other animal can do: we could limit ourselves voluntarily, *choose* to remain God's creatures instead of making ourselves gods. What a towering achievement that would be, so much more impressive than the largest dam (beavers can build dams) because so much harder. Such restraint—not genetic engineering or planetary management—is the real challenge, the hard thing. Of course we can splice genes. But can we *not* splice genes?

The momentum behind our impulse to control nature may be too strong to stop. But the likelihood of defeat is not an excuse to avoid trying. In one sense it's an aesthetic choice we face, much like Thoreau's, though what is at stake is less the shape of our own lives than the very practical question of the lives of all the other species and the creation they together constitute. But it is, of course, for our benefit, too. Jeffers wrote, "Integrity is wholeness, the greatest beauty is / organic wholeness of life and things, the divine beauty of the universe. Love that, not man / Apart from that, or else you will share man's pitiful confusions, or drown in despair when his days darken." The day has come when we choose between that wholeness and man in it or man apart, between that old clarity or new darkness.

The strongest reason for choosing man apart is, as I have said, the idea that nature has ended. And I think it has. But I cannot stand the clanging finality of the argument I've made, any more than people have ever been able to stand the clanging finality of their own deaths. So I hope against hope. Though not in our time, and not in the time of our children, or their children, if we now, *today*, limited our numbers and our desires and our ambitions, perhaps nature could someday resume its independent working. Perhaps the temperature could someday adjust itself to its own setting, and the rain fall of its own accord.

Time, as I said at the start of this essay, is elusive, odd. Perhaps the ten thousand years of our encroaching, defiant civilization, an eternity to us and a yawn to the rocks around us, could give way to ten thousand years of humble civilization when we choose to pay more for the benefits of nature, when we rebuild the sense of wonder and sanctity that could protect the natural world. At the end of that span we would still be so young, and perhaps ready to revel in the timelessness that surrounds us. I said, much earlier, that one of the possible meanings of the end of nature is that God is dead.

But another, if there was or is any such thing as God, is that he has granted us free will and now looks on, with great concern and love, to see how we exercise it: to see if we take the chance offered by this crisis to bow down and humble ourselves, or if we compound original sin with terminal sin.

AND IF WHAT I FEAR indeed happens? If the next twenty years sees us pump ever more gas into the sky, and if it sees us take irrevocable steps into the genetically engineered future, what solace then? The only ones in need of consolation will be those of us who were born in the transitional decades, too early to adapt completely to a brave new ethos.

I've never paid more than the usual attention to the night sky, perhaps because I grew up around cities, on suburban blocks lined with streetlights. But last August, on a warm Thursday afternoon, my wife and I hauled sleeping bags high into the mountains and laid them out on a rocky summit and waited for night to fall and the annual Perseid meteor shower to begin. After midnight, it finally started in earnest—every minute, every thirty seconds, another spear of light shot across some corner of the sky, so fast that unless you were looking right at it you had only the sense of a flash. Our bed was literally rock-hard, and when, toward dawn, an unforecast rain soaked our tentless clearing, it was cold—but the night was glorious, and I've since gotten a telescope. When, in *Paradise Lost*, Adam asks about the movements of the heavens, Raphael refuses to answer. "Let it speak," he says, "the Maker's high magnificence, who built / so spacious, and his line stretcht out so far; / That man may know he dwells not in his own; / An edifice too large for him to fill, / Lodg'd in a small partition, and the rest / Ordain'd for uses to his Lord best known." We may be creating microscopic nature; we may have altered the middle nature all around us; but this vast nature above our atmosphere still holds mystery and wonder. The occasional satellite does blip across, but it is almost a self-parody. Someday, man may figure out a method of conquering the stars, but at least for now when we look into the night sky, it is as Burroughs said: "We do not see ourselves reflected there—we are swept away from ourselves, and impressed with our own insignificance."

As I lay on the mountaintop that August night I tried to pick out the few constellations I could identify—Orion's Belt, the Dippers. The ancients, surrounded by wild and even hostile nature, took comfort in seeing the familiar above them—spoons and swords and nets. But we will need to train ourselves not to see those patterns. The comfort we need is inhuman.

Index

About the Author

BILL McKIBBEN has written about the natural world for publications ranging from *The New York Review of Books* and *The New York Times* to *Outside* and *Rolling Stone*. A former staff writer for *The New Yorker*, he has written many books on the media and environment. He lives with his wife and daughter in the Adirondack mountains of New York State.